BOY V. GIRL?

HOW GENDER SHAPES WHO WE ARE,
WHAT WE WANT, AND HOW WE GET ALONG

BOY V. GIRL?

HOW GENDER SHAPES WHO WE ARE,
WHAT WE WANT, AND HOW WE GET ALONG

George Abrahams, Ph.D., and Sheila Ahlbrand

Edited by Marjorie Lisovskis

free spirit
PUBLiSHiNG®

Works
for kids®

Library of Congress Cataloging-in-Publication Data
Abrahams, George, 1951–
　　Boy v. girl? : how gender shapes who we are, what we want, and how we get along / George Abrahams and Sheila Ahlbrand.
　　　　p. cm.
　　Includes bibliographical references and index.
　　ISBN 1-57542-104-6
　　　　1. Sex role—Juvenile literature. 2. Gender identity—Juvenile literature. 3. Sex (Psychology)—Juvenile literature. 4. Adolescent psychology—Juvenile literature. I. Title: Boy versus girl?. II. Ahlbrand, Sheila, 1965–　III. Title.

HQ1075 .A22 2002
305.3—dc21   2002003880

At the time of this book's publication, all facts and figures cited are the most current available; all telephone numbers, addresses, and Web site URLs are accurate and active; all publications, organizations, Web sites, and other resources exist as described in this book; and all have been verified. The authors and Free Spirit Publishing make no warranty or guarantee concerning the information and materials given out by organizations or content found at Web sites, and we are not responsible for any changes that occur after this book's publication. If you find an error or believe that a resource listed here is not as described, please contact Free Spirit Publishing. Parents, teachers, and other adults: We strongly urge you to monitor children's use of the Internet.

Cover and interior design by Marieka Heinlen
Index by Kay K. Schlembach

10 9 8 7 6 5 4 3 2 1
Printed in the United States of America

Free Spirit Publishing Inc.
217 Fifth Avenue North, Suite 200
Minneapolis, MN 55401-1299
(612) 338-2068
help4kids@freespirit.com
www.freespirit.com

The following are registered trademarks of Free Spirit Publishing Inc.:

FREE SPIRIT®
FREE SPIRIT PUBLISHING®
SELF-HELP FOR TEENS®
SELF-HELP FOR KIDS®
WORKS FOR KIDS®
THE FREE SPIRITED CLASSROOM®

In memory of my brother, Steve, and father, Donald Abrahams, whose playfulness, courage, and gentle presence continue to be a source of guidance and comfort. —G.A.

To the strong women of the Upper Midwest Women's History Center, mentors and friends, whose lives are testament to all the things that women can do. —S.A.

Acknowledgments

We are deeply grateful to the following people who helped to make this book possible:

Judy Galbraith, for her belief in this book.

Marjorie Lisovskis, for her astute editorial input, guidance, and generous sense of collaboration.

The staff of Free Spirit Publishing, especially Jennifer Brannen, April Fox, Darsi Dreyer, Douglas Fehlen, Nancy Robinson, and Elizabeth Verdick, who all contributed greatly in editorial matters as well as with the survey, and Marieka Heinlen for her creative work on the design and illustrations.

All the young people who completed our survey, who provided valuable insight and reminded us of the importance of asking questions and listening to the answers.

Elizabeth Peterson, for her close reading of early drafts of the book.

Susan Gross and the Upper Midwest Women's History Center, for their tireless work in the field of women's and gender issues and for their early support of this work.

Our families:

Skinner, who always offers support and a reminder to take time to have fun.

Anna, for her help in distributing surveys and for always demonstrating that life is exponentially richer by embracing the full range of possibilities.

Jacob, whose generous and playful spirit is a daily reminder to enjoy the moment and be open to all that comes your way.

Marty, who has read every version of this book and is a constant source of support and joy.

CONTENTS

LIST OF REPRODUCIBLE PAGES

INTRODUCTION

"Boys have it easy!
They can do what they want, when they want!" Girl, 16

"Girls can get away with anything." Boy, 14

These are comments from two middle-school students who filled out a survey about what being a girl or a boy meant to them in their everyday lives. Some teens (and adults) feel that there's a big difference between what boys and girls can do or be. Why? Because, as another girl who answered the survey wrote, "We grow up thinking that boys are supposed to do certain things and girls are supposed to do certain things."

From the moment you were born and somebody announced, "It's a boy!" or "It's a girl!", society has been sending you messages about the way it expects you to look, think, and behave. These messages come at you from all directions—parents, TV, magazines, music, movies, books, newspapers, toys, teachers, even your friends. You've probably been told things like:

Girls are delicate—boys are strong.

Boys never say anything—girls talk too much.

Girls are emotional—boys can't/don't/won't show their feelings.

Boys fight—girls gossip.

You probably know from your personal experience that these things aren't always true. But still, many people seem to believe they are—or that they *should* be. We wanted to find out what teenagers thought about the ideas, so we surveyed nearly 2,000 middle-school teens about what being a

1

girl or a boy meant to them in their everyday lives. (You'll find the surveys, one for boys and one for girls, on pages 172–179.) We asked what students liked—and didn't like—about being a girl or a boy. We asked if they thought rules and expectations at home were fair. We asked how they felt about the way teachers and other school officials treated them and about how female and male teens are portrayed in magazines, on TV, and in the movies.

The students who took the survey had a lot to say about what society and individuals expect from boys and girls. One boy told us, "Popular culture affects people, but other girls and guys affect people even more. It's a competition."

Which made us wonder . . .

Is it really a "boy v. girl" world?

Is life really a boys-against-the-girls kind of deal? Do teens think of themselves as girls or boys first, and people second? If so, is that what boys and girls want? If not, what's really going on?

This book is a place where you can start to sort some of these things out. *Boy v. Girl?* challenges you to look beyond the assumptions people often make about what it means to be one sex or the other. People make assumptions when they think they know who you are based on what you look like, how you talk, who you spend time with, where you live, or what sex you are. If you're like most people, you don't like to have assumptions made about you. It's frustrating when people judge you based on superficial information. With this book, you'll have a chance to explore your own ideas of who you are and who you want to become and to make decisions based on what you believe is right for *you*.

About this book

There are lots of books about girls for girls, or about boys for boys, or about girls for boys, or about boys for girls. Many of them have great insight and advice on what it means to be one or the other. But we're all human beings. Both boys and girls have to deal with situations and experiences that make it hard for them to be who they want to be as individuals. And everyone needs to figure out how to get along with people of both sexes at school, at home, and in relationships. That's why we wrote this book for girls *and* boys. It has some information that's specific for boys and some that's specific for girls, but most of what you'll read will be of use to everyone.

One thing that stood out in the surveys is that girls and boys really want to know what's going on with people of the other sex. They want to understand and they want to *be* understood. Reading *Boy v. Girl?* can help you see things from both views, boys' and girls'. It can show you a middle ground, a place where you'll see some of the ways teenagers of both sexes are more alike than different. We hope it will help you find the truth behind the mixed messages that surround you so you can let experience and knowledge, not assumptions, guide you.

Throughout *Boy v. Girl?* you'll see

* quotes from people who took the survey, telling you how they feel about the different issues the book talks about

* interesting (and sometimes fun) facts about how girls and boys are alike and different

* conversation or writing starters called "What do you think?" to help you sort through what you're wondering and feeling as you explore the book's ideas

* surveys and activity sheets to photocopy and fill out by yourself, with friends, or with your family

* lists of books, Web sites, and organizations where you can find out more about topics that interest you

A word about the words we use

In *Boy v. Girl?*, we talk about the other sex instead of the opposite sex. That's because we think other leaves room for all those ways the sexes are alike rather than different.

And since boys and girls have many things in common, it was important to us to write about the two sexes in as similar a way as possible. One thing we thought about was using the term guys instead of boys. A lot of people think of boys as guys—the trouble is, there's really no similar term for girls that's kind of casual but doesn't label the girl. For example, "grrrrl" sounds like a girl who wants to be considered tough or assertive, though "guy" doesn't necessarily mean that. In the end, we decided to call teen girls *girls* and teen boys *boys, most of the time.* It seemed logical, fair, and straightforward.

Boy v. Girl? tries to emphasize that everyone is an individual and that it's important to be true to who you are. Being male or female is just one piece of the puzzle. Some of the other things that make you *you* include the color of your skin, how old you are, where you live, what kind of a family you have, and your own personal views and feelings. So when you read this book, realize that because it was written for all kinds of young people, it might sometimes talk about things that don't fit your particular situation. You might not have any brothers or sisters, or you might have lots of them. You might live with two parents or one, or you might live with a relative or in a foster home. You might have friends of your own sex, the other sex, or both.

No matter what your situation, this book is meant to give you a chance to find the freedom to be you—to be different if you want to be—and to develop the tools to feel confident about yourself. Use the ideas that work for you and who you are. You're the best person to decide that.

We'd like to hear your feelings about being a teen boy or girl. We'd also like to know what parts of this book were especially interesting or helpful to you. So please write to us at this address:

George Abrahams and Sheila Ahlbrand
c/o Free Spirit Publishing Inc.
217 Fifth Avenue North, Suite 200
Minneapolis, MN 55401-1299

Or email us at:
help4kids@freespirit.com

For us, *Boy v. Girl?* has been a journey. We hope it will be one for you, too. Take your time with it. Read it on your own or with a friend. Have fun.

George Abrahams & Sheila Ahlbrand

Chapter I

WHAT IN THE WORLD IS GENDER, ANYWAY?

SURVEY COMMENTS:
How did teens define the term GENDER?

"Female or male (circle one)." —Boy, 13

"Gender means a separation of boys and girls." —Girl, 12

"It's a difference—one way of categorizing people." —Girl, 12

"It's the person you are. How you act. What you look like. What sex you are." —Boy, 14

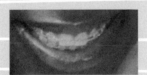

"Gender means human." —Girl, 13

"It's the way your chromosomes are aligned." —Boy, 13

"Gender to me means who you are, what you've done, how you feel about yourself—not if you're a boy or a girl. It goes much deeper than that." —Girl, 14

"Gender is the difference between girl and guy." —Boy, 13

"It's about the opposite sex." —Girl, 12

"It's whether you're a dude or a chick." —Boy, 16

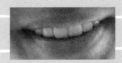

"To me it's a boundary between two different worlds." —Girl, 12

"Gender means sex, hormones, what you are expected to do in the world." —Boy, 14

Does gender = sex?

You know that this book is about what it means to be a girl or a boy today, and that it's got something to do with gender. What is gender anyway? This was the very first question on our survey, and most people said something like "it means you're a boy or a girl" or "it's about being female or male" or "it means what sex you are." Actually, gender and sex mean different things.

Ancient Roman symbol of Mars—represents the male

Sex is about biology and body parts. If you were born with one set of parts you're considered male, and if you were born with another set of parts you're considered female. (For more about those "parts," see pages 18–21.)

Gender is about what you (and others) think, feel, and expect of people *based on* what sex they are. There are certain traits and ways of behaving that are considered feminine and others that are considered masculine. Each person's ideas about what's masculine and what's feminine are different, but there are basic views that groups of people share. For example, in many countries, including Canada and the United States, some of the things typically seen as feminine include caring for others, talking about feelings, and showing emotions. Some of the things generally considered masculine involve taking charge, being strong, and thinking logically. We call these ideas about what's usually expected from women or girls and from men or boys *gender roles*.

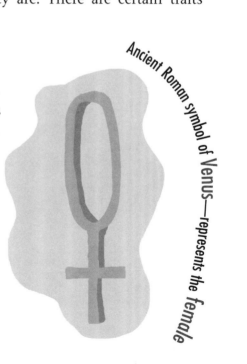

Ancient Roman symbol of Venus—represents the female

Where do gender roles come from?

One place gender roles come from is society—the people in a country or community. To some extent, every society has traditions and rules about how males and females are expected to be, think, and act. Maybe you've heard these old nursery rhymes about boys and girls:

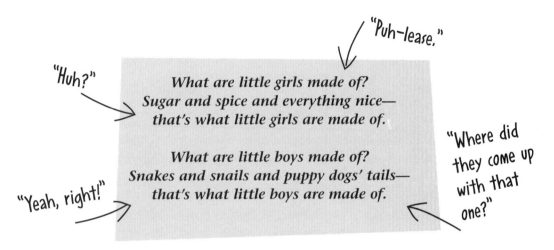

"Huh?"

"Puh-lease."

What are little girls made of?
Sugar and spice and everything nice—
that's what little girls are made of.

What are little boys made of?
Snakes and snails and puppy dogs' tails—
that's what little boys are made of.

"Yeah, right!"

"Where did they come up with that one?"

Okay, we all know that girls aren't about sugar and spice; boys aren't made of reptiles and dog parts either. But is there a kernel of truth to these silly rhymes? Is there something sweeter and softer about girls? Something rougher and tougher about boys?

On the day you were born, it's likely that somebody—maybe a nurse or your mom or dad—put you in a pink hat or blanket to show that you were a girl, or a blue one to show that you were a boy. And think about those Saturday morning shows you used to watch as a kid (maybe you still watch them). Ever notice the commercials for toys that played over and over again? Today, as then, the ads mostly show girls playing with fashion dolls, kitchen sets, and makeup mirrors, and boys playing with toy guns, video games, and miniature cars. When you were younger, you got the media message that girls prefer dolls and other sweet, pink stuff, while boys like things that are violent or make lots of noise.

Even though society plays a big part in creating and influencing gender roles, you play a part, too. Like all people, you form your own ideas about gender based on your personal experiences. These ideas depend on many things, including

* ✳ where you grew up

* ✳ who you grew up with

* ✳ the things your parents and other people in your family believe and tell you

* ✳ what religious values and rules you learned

* ✳ how your friends think and act

* ✳ your own inner feelings, beliefs, and expectations about what it means to be a girl or a boy

Gender roles may not be as clear-cut as those TV ads want you to think they are! Your ideas about gender roles are unique. You might be a girl who loves to use makeup, or you may think the only thing eye shadow and blush are good for is clogging pores. You could be a boy who lives for the day you can race fast cars, or you might find cars and machinery boring. Or maybe you're a boy *or* a girl who loves to play—and win—video games just as much as you like to cook, or illustrate your own comic books, or try new ways to fix hair.

One of the questions we asked in our survey was what people liked and didn't like about being a girl or a boy. Teens had lots to say about this, and you'll read their comments throughout the book. Many of the remarks show (1) that society *does* shape people's ideas about gender roles and (2) that individuals see gender roles differently. Here are a few things people wrote.

THE SURVEY ASKED:

What are the best and worst things about being a girl or a boy?

GIRLS SAID:

"The best part of being a girl: I can cry whenever I want. The worst part: people think I'm weak and ditzy."

"I guess I like being a girl, because I can be peaceful and nice and not fight like a lot of boys do. But I don't like it when people care how I look and dress."

"Most people think girls are sweet, but I don't think I am."

"I like doing girly things (shopping, makeup, clothes, hair, the movies, etc.)."

"We can play guys' sports, but if guys play girls' sports, that's a bigger deal."

"I like to climb trees, and people tell me that's boy stuff."

"I love being a girl. I can do anything. Like boys worry about if something is too 'girly' and they avoid it, where a girl won't have to worry."

BOYS SAID:

"What's best about being a boy? You're smarter, stronger, faster."

"Boys always have to be tough, where girls can be sensitive. I would like to show my emotions, too."

"People think you have to be the tough figure."

"I like playing sports like football."

"There is a lot of pressure to do 'manly' things."

"You're strong, but people think you're bad."

"There are things I want to change, like all the peer pressure, but being a boy has more adrenaline involved, so it's more fun."

WHAT DO YOU THINK?

Some of the things you'll read about in *Boy v. Girl?* will probably get you thinking about what's going on in your own life. We've included some questions to help you sort through what you're wondering and feeling. You can deal with these questions in whatever way you want. Write about the questions in your journal, think about them while you're on the bus or hanging out at home, or talk about them with a friend.

✱ What's the best thing for *you* about being a girl or a boy? What's the worst thing?

✱ What are some ways gender roles affect your life?

THE SURVEY SAID:
82% of boys said they liked being a boy.
82% of girls said they liked being a girl.

Even though people's ideas about gender roles differ in many ways, there seem to be certain social "rules"—things you're "supposed" to do if you're a boy or a girl. The clothes you wear, how and whether you use makeup or jewelry, and the activities you choose in and out of school send signals to the rest of the world about your gender role. They fit society's image of being either masculine or feminine.

What are the gender roles in your life? Try this activity on your own or with a friend: Take a piece of paper and fold it in half vertically. At the top of one folded side write, "Where I live, girls are 'supposed' to . . ." On the other side write, "Where I live, boys are 'supposed' to . . ." Then make two lists of the gender "rules" you think come from society. When you're done, unfold the paper and look at the lists side by side. Are there similarities? Differences? Make additional lists about the gender roles at home, at school, in your group of friends, and for other situations. Which ideas do you agree with? Which *don't* you agree with?

At the mall, girls are "supposed" to:

Many of the activities and experiences we may typically consider "boy things" and "girl things" can be fun. The question isn't whether you should or shouldn't like to act, think, and feel in certain ways. The question is: Do you want to let what *others* expect pressure you into acting, thinking, or feeling in certain ways? Fitting into a strict gender role can be like trying to fit into a shirt you don't like. You can wear it, but it doesn't feel right.

WHAT DO YOU THINK?

* Have you ever thought about yourself as being more than "a boy" or "a girl"? How could thinking beyond those labels lead you to feel differently about yourself?

* What are your personal expectations of the boys and girls you meet? How do you feel when other people judge you with the same kinds of expectations?

When gender roles = stereotypes

If you think gender roles sound a lot like stereotypes, you're on to something. Gender and stereotypes often seem to go hand in hand. What exactly is a stereotype? Let's take a quick look at the dictionary definition.

ster·e·o·type (stereotype) *n.* 1. a conventional, formulaic, and usually oversimplified conception, opinion, or belief. 2. A person, group, event, or issue considered to typify or conform to an unvarying pattern or manner, lacking any individuality. — *tr.v.* **-typed, -typing, -types.** 1. To develop a fixed, unvarying idea about. 2. To make a stereotype of.

Conventional. Formulaic. Conform. Unvarying. B-O-R-I-N-G! Don't these words make you wonder why anyone would ever want to be stereotyped?

More briefly put, a stereotype is a general and oversimplified view that all people in a group are the same in some way. It's hard to live in our world and not know about stereotypes. People get stereotyped because of

* their age
* the color of their skin
* how much money they have
* their religion
* their athletic ability
* the clothes they wear

* the way they talk
* the people they're friends with
* how they perform in school
* the activities they like to do
* the foods they eat
* and so on and so on and so on

Where do stereotypes come from?

Often stereotypes are based on someone's personal experience. If that experience was bad, the stereotype is negative. Here's an example. Say you're walking down the street and someone with an orange shirt calls you a name. A few minutes later a different person in an orange shirt shoves you out of line at the store. So you decide that people with orange shirts are mean. Later in the day a person with an orange shirt smiles at you and offers you a seat on the bus, but you ignore this person because you're pretty sure people with orange shirts are mean. The person on the bus could actually be very nice, but you've missed the chance to get acquainted because of the stereotype you've formed.

That may seem like a silly example, but stereotypes can be silly, too. In fact, anything that causes you to pass up a chance to make a new friend because you've stereotyped the person without giving her or him a chance is more than silly. It's sad.

Gender stereotypes assume people will behave or think in certain ways based simply on what sex they are. Sometimes people think that gender is like two boxes—kind of like those boxes you check for male or female. They want to put all the traits that make you masculine in one box and all the traits that make you feminine in the other. The things that get stuffed in those two boxes are gender stereotypes—traits that are considered true for all boys or for all girls.

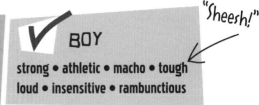

When someone assumes a girl isn't strong enough to lift something heavy but a boy is, that's a gender stereotype. If you hear someone say, "Girls love to gossip" or "Boys are rowdy," these are gender stereotypes. "Wait," you might say. "I know a girl who loves to gossip, and I know a boy who's really wild." Even so, not all girls gossip, and not all boys are rowdy. The problem with gender stereotypes is that they can keep people from really knowing and understanding each other.

A lot of teens who answered the survey said they tried not to stereotype other people because it was mean. One boy wrote, "When I'm stereotyped, I feel like people don't want to know me, but rather choose someone else to represent me." A girl who had been stereotyped said, "I felt like someone had just taken my pride away." Another student wrote, "When I've been stereotyped, I've felt cheated. If someone judges my appearance without knowing me, it's unfair." Another said simply, "Stereotypes hurt." Here are some other things the boys and girls in the survey said about gender stereotypes.

THE SURVEY ASKED:

Have you ever been stereotyped, or stereotyped someone else, because of being a boy or a girl?

BOYS SAID:

"I have my ear pierced two times. Because I'm a boy, most people look at me and think I am a punk, a rebel, or I'm mean. Actually the reason I pierced my ear was a sign of friendship with my two best friends."

GIRLS SAID:

"I have been stereotyped for being a blonde! But I'm not DUMB. It is so embarrassing because I know I'm not dumb, but that's what people automatically assume."

BOYS SAID:

"People think that if you're a boy, you like to fist-fight. I hate fist-fighting."

"I was stereotyped for being a boy when I was told that I couldn't have a certain haircut."

"Yes, people said boys don't have a sweet side."

"Girls sometimes think I'm just a stupid jock."

"Boys at my age are classified as 'horny and horny.'"

"You can never cry or show emotion, and you have to be buff and macho."

"Sometimes I call guys 'girls' to take away their manhood."

GIRLS SAID:

"If you play sports people seem to think of you as a tomboy. We are still girls if we aren't a cheerleader."

"Guys think they can walk all over me because I'm a girl. They think I'm weak."

"I have had people come up to me and say girls should be quiet and not state their opinion."

"People say that maybe if a girl has big breasts she is considered a slut, but if a guy has big muscles he is a jock."

"Sometimes I do stereotype people, as a sudden reaction to anger or fear."

"Usually boys aren't very smart, so I tease them about that."

"I don't like it when I get stereotyped. Why should I stereotype others?"

THE SURVEY SAID:

39% of boys said they have been stereotyped because they are a boy.

61% of girls said they have been stereotyped because they are a girl.

27% of boys said they have stereotyped others because they are boys or girls.

28% of girls said they have stereotyped others because they are girls or boys.

WHAT DO YOU THINK?

* Think of some stereotypes about girls and boys. Which do you believe are true? Which aren't? Why?

* Have you ever been stereotyped or stereotyped someone because of being a boy or a girl? How did it feel?

* Can stereotypes ever be positive? Why or why not?

Double whammies

If a stereotype based on one thing, like gender, can be untrue and hurtful, then a stereotype based on two things has the possibility of being twice as untrue and hurtful. Some of the teens who answered our survey brought this up in regard to race. One boy told us that being stereotyped in this way made him feel like he was an alien. A girl wrote, "I feel bad, because you can't change your ethnic background or being a girl." Other people said, "It made me wish I was someone else" and "I thought it was really unfair and mean."

The truth is that each person is a complicated individual. Stereotyping someone is quick—all it takes is a glance. And it's easier than actually taking a risk and making the effort to get to know the person. When you stereotype someone, you trick yourself into thinking you know or understand the person when you really don't.

It may not be easy, but the best way to keep from stereotyping someone is to look at the person as an individual, rather than at the person's sex (or race, or color, or religion, or whatever). The first step to doing this is to *not* make assumptions about people because of their sex, race, or anything else.

That goes for your expectations of yourself, too. There's a lot of pressure to show certain traits and do certain activities because as a girl or a boy you're "supposed" to. But think how good it feels to simply be yourself! You can free yourself from gender stereotyping. You can get to know who you are, be comfortable with that person, and be open to trying new things. You can make a conscious choice to respect other people so they can do the same. Then the idea of gender might become less important than the idea of being *you*.

"Gender doesn't matter, it's about the person inside." Girl, 13

Find out more!

Free to Be . . . You and Me by Marlo Thomas and friends. Wait! We know you're not eight years old anymore! But this recording (on CD, video, or DVD) is a classic, worth revisiting if you remember it from when you were younger, and worth discovering if you missed it back then. It's a funny, down-to-earth look at who and what boys and girls *can* be. There's also a book by the same name (Philadelphia: Running Press, 1998).

Gender Issues by Kaye Stearman and Nikki van der Gaag (Austin, TX: Raintree Steck-Vaughn, 1996). This is a short, interesting, easy-to-read book that looks at how gender issues affect the lives of people all over the world and how gender roles are changing. Since it's a book written to be used in school, your best bet for finding it might be to check with a librarian or an online bookstore.

More Than a Label: Why What You Wear or Who You're With Doesn't Define Who You Are by Aisha Muharrar (Minneapolis: Free Spirit Publishing, 2002). A seventeen-year-old author looks at labels, cliques, peer pressure, popularity, racism, sexism, and more in this book about how stereotypes and labels hurt and limit people in high school. Like *Boy v. Girl?*, *More Than a Label* includes student survey responses.

Chapter 2

ARE GIRLS AND BOYS REALLY SO DIFFERENT?

SURVEY COMMENTS:

What did teens say about the differences between boys and girls?

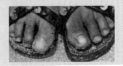 "Intellectually: they're the same. Emotionally: girls are more emotional. Physically: guys are better at sports." —Boy, 15

"Boys don't play with dolls, and girls don't play with cars." —Girl, 11

"Men are supposed to be the leaders." —Boy, 12

"There is no difference between us except physical features." —Girl, 14

"I think what boys lack girls have, and what girls lack boys have." —Boy, 14

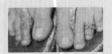

"Girls can do anything boys can." —Girl, 13

"We both have to deal with dumb problems." —Girl, 13

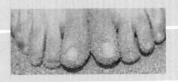

"I've learned that girls are capable of beating me in academics and sports, so I see us as equal." —Boy, 12

"Boys are higher because history places them there." —Boy, 14

"Boys and girls are both people and they both have feelings and opinions." —Boy, 14

"We all have strengths and weaknesses." —Girl, 13

"We're alike because we're all humans. Most of us." —Girl, 13

"Girls would not survive alone in this world, and neither would boys." —Boy, 13

Puberty brings differences front and center

If gender is based on the way people see the differences between the sexes, it's worth taking a look at what those differences are. A lot of fuss is made about how different boys and girls and men and women are from each other. But what exactly is different? And what's the same?

Body parts

What's different?

These parts are unique to girls or boys:

GIRLS	BOYS
clitoris and vagina	penis
ovaries	testicles
vulva	scrotum

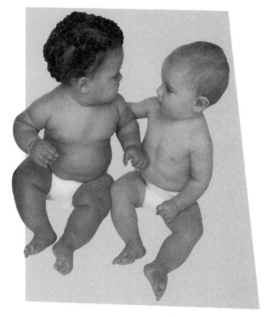

What's the same?

Both girls and boys have these parts:

eyes	ears
nose	mouth
arms	hands
fingers	chest
abdomen	legs
feet	toes

You get the idea. Girls and boys have a lot more the same than they do different. Still, there are differences even in the ways male and female bodies are the same. Males are generally taller, heavier, and stronger than females, plus they have less body fat. Obviously all males aren't taller, heavier, and stronger than all females. And some boys *and* girls have smaller feet, or bigger hands, or shorter legs, or longer arms. Chests and breasts come in a variety of shapes and sizes. So do noses and ears, toes and fingers.

Those body parts that are different can have a tremendous effect on how you experience the world. Right now your body may be going through many changes. You may find that you compare yourself to others and the ways they're changing. When you look at people of the same sex, it's hard not to ask yourself things like, "Am I the only person who . . . ?" or "Why does everybody else seem to be . . . ?" or "Am I abnormal?"

The truth is that there is no "normal" way for changes to take place. Bodies change on different timetables. If you feel like you're changing too fast or too slow, it might be because of how the world around you *thinks* you should grow or look because you are either a girl or a boy. The sooner you start to grow and change, the sooner people are likely to treat you more like an adult. The other side is true, too: the later body changes occur, the longer it may take for some people to treat you as grown-up.

Sometimes you'll find people reacting to changes they see in your body that have nothing to do with who you are inside. Changing earlier or later than most of your friends can be hard for anyone. When boys or girls appear physically mature, people sometimes expect them to act and think like grown-ups rather than like preteens and teens who are in the process of becoming young adults. Some kids may feel ready for the responsibility that comes with this, while others may not. The pressures that come with puberty can affect girls and boys in different ways.

♀ **Girls' view:** If a girl starts to develop breasts early, people tend to look at her differently than they did before. Sometimes they really *look* at her differently. A number of girls who answered our survey complained that when boys talked to them, they looked at their breasts instead of their faces. Many times, just because a girl has breasts, people start to think of her as a woman before she may feel that way. This can be really difficult to deal with. People begin to expect things that have more to do with her body than with who she is as a person. It can also be hard for girls who develop breasts later or whose breasts are smaller. Often people view a girl with small breasts or hips as "just a kid."

These expectations can happen when it comes to menstruation, too. Among girls, beginning to menstruate is a pretty big deal, and it happens on very different timetables. A girl who's started menstruating might feel uncomfortable to have other girls notice; a girl who hasn't started yet might feel equally embarrassed. Whatever their stage of physical development, girls can be stereotyped by adults, friends, and even themselves, just because of how they look or what's going on with their bodies.

♂ **Boys' view:** Society in general has decided that the most masculine men are tall and strong, so boys who mature early often are likely to be more accepted and respected. When a boy becomes tall and muscular at an early age, people begin to see him more like a man—as someone to take seriously. The opposite of tall and muscular is short and skinny, so if tall and muscular is considered masculine, short and skinny is seen as something less than masculine. There are other issues for boys as well. In the survey, boys talked about being judged by other boys based on the size of their penis. And by the end of middle school, some boys have started to shave while others haven't. Some boys' voices have deepened while others' have not yet changed. All these physical differences can be a source of embarrassment for boys.

Author William S. Pollack interviewed hundreds of teenage boys for his book *Real Boys' Voices*. In the book, Pollack talks about what he calls The Boy Code: an unwritten set of rules that boys feel they have to live by. He says that appearing weak or feminine is the biggest no-no in The Boy Code. If a boy is smaller than the other boys his age, he's probably going to get harassed for it. That could mean name-calling and teasing or even being physically harmed— sometimes by those boys who've matured early. (For more information on harassment, see pages 90–96.)

By now you may be thinking something like

Aaaaaarrggghh! Do things **really** have to be so complicated?

Do sex and gender really have to get in the way of how I see myself and other people?

The answer is: Only if you let them. *You* can decide what you want to expect from yourself and others. A great starting point for thinking about, setting, or changing expectations is to try to understand what other people are going through. In other words, empathize. This isn't hard to do when someone's experiencing the same changes as you. If you're a boy with a big pimple on your nose and you've been hiding your face with your hand all day, you can empathize with the girl next to you who's trying to cover the zit on her forehead with her hair. Or if you're a really tall girl who stands several inches above the shortest boy in your class, you can look at each other and realize that you both feel pretty awkward.

But it's a little tougher when it comes to those changes that boys and girls don't share. While it may be impossible to *completely* understand the changes that happen to the other sex, you can learn as much as possible about them and try to imagine how it would feel to be going through them.

Hormones send the signals

Hormones guide many of your body's processes—things like your physical growth, your sexual development, and your blood pressure. You can think of hormones as chemical messengers that travel through the bloodstream. Their job is to signal different cells in the body to react in specific ways.

There are all kinds of hormones, but the ones that are important to this book are the sex hormones, which manage the changes that take place in your body during puberty. They are responsible for many of the differences between males and females.

Hormones send signals like:

"Hey, let's make sure this guy's voice cracks during his social studies report!"

"Pump up that blood pressure—she's gotta kick a field goal!"

Sex hormones during puberty

What's different?

BOYS

- hormones are produced in the testicles
- male hormones are called androgens
- main hormone is testosterone
- testosterone goes up and down daily

GIRLS

- hormones are produced in the ovaries
- female hormones are called estrogens
- main hormone is estradiol
- estradiol goes up and down monthly

What's the same?

- hormones travel to different parts of the body, carrying the message that it's time for sexual development to begin
- both males and females make and use testosterone and estradiol, but men have ten times more testosterone in their bloodstream than women, and women have ten times more estradiol than men

Hormones can sometimes make girls and boys feel like they've completely lost all control over what their bodies are doing.

♂ Boys' view: Partly due to testosterone, boys' voices can "crack" or go up or down unexpectedly. They can get erections (hard-ons) at embarrassing moments. Boys may feel uncomfortable or ashamed about what their bodies are doing, or they may even be afraid that something is wrong with them. Lots of the boys in our survey didn't even want to talk about their bodies. We asked a question about how the differences in girls' and boys' bodies affect who they are, and many boys wrote things like "None of your business!" and "Private!"

♀ Girls' view: For girls, estrogen controls their periods. Some girls are excited to have their period, because it means that they're "officially" women. Sometimes girls feel embarrassed, worried, frightened, or even ashamed about menstruation. Many of the girls who answered our survey said that getting their period was the thing they liked least about being a girl. Along with their period, girls may also experience cramps, headaches, stomachaches, backaches, skin breakouts, weight gain, irritability, moodiness, and even depression brought on by hormonal surges. These things aren't exactly fun!

WHAT DO YOU THINK?

✱ How do you feel about the changes you're experiencing during puberty?

✱ Why do you think some girls and boys feel embarrassed or ashamed about their bodies?

Feeling and dealing with emotions

One person who took the survey wrote, "Girls get crabby once a month." Sometimes people tease a girl who is upset or moody and blame it on menstruation. If you're a boy, think for a minute about all the things that happen to a girl's body during the menstrual cycle. You might get crabby, too, if you got cramps and put on weight every month.

On the other hand, just because a girl is in a bad mood doesn't mean it's because of her period. And boys have emotions, too. During puberty, lots of boys experience anger. One reason for this might be because testosterone controls anger and aggressiveness. Testosterone levels go up and down several times daily, so a boy's emotions can change frequently during the day.

Anger is a strong emotion, and it can be a confusing one. Everyone gets angry—it's only human. And while anger can be an issue for boys during puberty, it's something both boys and girls experience. Anger can come on quickly or simmer and grow over time. Screaming and yelling, punching, refusing to speak, spreading rumors, and making nasty remarks are all expressions of anger. But they're negative expressions. It may sound funny, but there are positive things you can do to deal with anger. Here are a few ideas for you to try:

* **Calm down.** Do something physical. If you feel like hitting or lashing out, release that energy without hurting anyone. How? Find a private place where you can scream as loud as you want. Or run around outside, do some karate kicks, work up a sweat with aerobics, dance, or just jump up and down. You can also calm down by counting slowly to ten (or a hundred) and doing some deep breathing.

* **Write or talk about how you feel.** Writing can be a great way to both release strong feelings and think through why you're angry, what happened, and how you want to deal with it. If you're angry with another person, talking face-to-face once you've calmed down can help. To talk things through reasonably, it's important to keep from accusing or name-calling. Instead of saying, "You make me so mad!" try the trick of using an I-message. I-messages talk about how YOU feel and what YOU want: "When you make fun of me in front of people, I feel embarrassed. I really wish you wouldn't do that."

* **Look for the reasons and feelings behind your anger.** Sometimes anger seems to come from nowhere. But does it? Maybe you got a bad grade on a test and you're furious, but you're probably feeling other things underneath that anger. For example, you might be worried about passing the class, disappointed in yourself, or discouraged about how you did. Maybe you feel the teacher hasn't been fair to you. You'll more likely be able to solve the problem if you identify these things. Once you've released the strong anger of the moment,

you can start to figure out what to do (talk to the teacher? find a study partner?) so you don't feel worried, discouraged, or angry next time.

There's a lot of debate about how big a role things like hormones and body chemistry play in people's emotions. We know biology plays a role, but we also know that families, teachers, coaches, friends, and society in general send messages about the ways girls and boys are expected to deal with feelings. We asked about this in the survey, and students told us again and again that they got two clear messages from parents, teachers, and other young people:

1. Boys aren't supposed to cry—they're supposed to feel and act tough.

2. Girls are expected to cry and to talk about their feelings.

No matter what society seems to be telling you, you don't have to buy into this double standard. It's natural to sometimes feel angry, sad, frustrated, embarrassed, and confused. Girl *or* boy, it can really help to recognize the emotions you're experiencing, cry if you want to, and talk about how you feel with people who understand and care about you.

When emotions become too strong

If you're worried that your emotions are too extreme too much of the time, pay attention to your instincts. If other people are telling you that your anger, depression, or mood swings are getting out of control, listen to them. Find an adult who will help you figure out what's going on. If you feel like you just want to explode or give up, but you can't find someone to talk to, look in the Yellow Pages under Crisis Intervention for a help-line you can call, or call the toll-free National Youth Crisis Hotline: **1-800-448-4663.**

What about learning and thinking differences?

There's been growing interest in the past few years about the brain and how it works. One of the things researchers have looked at is what differences there are, or might be, between the male and female brain. Are girls' and boys' brains wired in completely different ways? No. Are there differences? Some. One is in the hormones that carry brain signals: the male brain is managed by a large amount of testosterone while the female brain is managed mainly by estrogen.

Researchers have found some differences in the ways boys and girls learn, think, and process information. Here are the main ones.

Thinking and solving problems

What's different?

GIRLS

- generally enjoy and do better at subjects and activities that involve language and verbal skills

- generally score better on verbal aptitude tests

- tend to use landmarks to navigate

- generally listen and solve problems with both sides of their brain

- tend to respond verbally

BOYS

- generally enjoy and do better at subjects and activities that involve math and spatial skills

- generally score better on math and science aptitude tests

- tend to use geography to navigate

- generally listen and solve problems with the left side of their brain

- tend to respond physically

What's the same?

No surprise: the differences apply generally, but not all the time. Some boys have strong language and verbal skills just like some girls are physical and do well in math.

Does this mean that boys' and girls' brains are biologically very different? Not necessarily. It may just be that males and females use their brains differently because of how they've been taught to behave over the years. (There are those stereotypes again!) Scientists and researchers don't agree about what the differences in thinking and learning mean. In fact, there's a lot of controversy about the differences between male and female brains.

New discoveries are made about the brain every day, so this is a question that will keep being explored. Though the majority of students we surveyed believed that girls and boys think differently, some strongly disagreed. Students' comments showed a variety of ideas about this.

THE SURVEY ASKED:
Do you think there are differences in how boys and girls think?

BOYS SAID:

"No one thinks alike, no matter if they are a boy or a girl."

"I do think there's a difference in how we think because of hormones and society."

"Girls mature faster and think different thoughts."

"Boys think about more things (like beating someone in basketball). Girls think more emotionally (like 'I hope I don't hurt her feelings')."

"Guys think about getting girls, and girls think about life and how they will turn out."

"Boys think more towards their performance and girls think more of their looks and beauty."

GIRLS SAID:

"Everything boys think, girls think the opposite."

"There are probably very little differences. It depends on the person's personality."

"Of course there are differences!"

"I think girls are more reasonable. They think more while boys give a quick answer."

"Girls think. Boys act."

"No. We're all human beings."

THE SURVEY SAID:

84% of boys believe there are differences in how boys and girls think.
86% of girls believe there are differences in how girls and boys think.

WHAT DO YOU THINK?

* Do boys and girls think differently? Explain your reasoning.

* If they do think differently, is that a positive or a negative thing? How important are the differences to you?

Do gender differences help or hurt us?

Girls and boys are different from each other, but they also have a lot in common. The differences can make life fun and interesting: Because of gender roles, you may feel like you know what to expect of someone, which can make it easier to relate. Sometimes, though, the roles we expect people to fit into can start to seem so important that we lose sight of the person inside. And, knowing we have so much more in common than we do different, how realistic are gender roles, anyway? Consider this:

Just suppose . . .

Suppose a friend of yours wants you to meet someone named Chris. The friend tells you Chris is a really good basketball player, has a great dog named Spike, and is kind of shy. You want to know more, so your friend tells you Chris is in the drama club and got in a fight last week after school. Is Chris a boy or a girl? How did you decide?

Do you think traits and interests are tied to gender roles? Page 32 has a "Gender traits?" form you can use to explore this idea some more. Photocopy the form. Then look at the list of words. Next to each word, write a "B" for boy or a "G" for girl. If you believe the trait applies to both boys and girls, write both a "B" and a "G." After you've marked all the words, go back and put a checkmark beside all the ones you think apply to you. Do any traits overlap? Go ahead and fill out the form now.

The point of thinking about these traits isn't to find out whether you're more feminine or masculine, but to show that there isn't necessarily always a clear line between one gender and the other. There's nothing wrong with having traits that are generally considered masculine *and* traits that are generally considered feminine. In fact, it's normal and desirable. Traits we typically think of as masculine often have to do with leadership, power, competitiveness, and aggression, while traits we typically call feminine have to do with kindness, communication, and helping others. Can you see why it might be a good thing to have both sets of traits? They help balance each other. When we expect people to behave like they have only "feminine" traits or "masculine" traits, we're not really thinking about them as a whole person.

WHAT DO YOU THINK?

Think of a situation where it might be desirable to

* be gutsy
* talk things through
* have patience

* take a stand
* be competitive
* show kindness

Crying at a sad movie doesn't make you less of a boy. Being an aggressive basketball player doesn't make you less of a girl. Remember those two boxes people sometimes use to stereotype girls and boys based on what sex they are (pages 12–13)? The truth is, most people have traits from both of those boxes, so saying you're either all masculine or all feminine just doesn't work. Where one boy or girl might like to compete in sports, another might not. Where one girl or boy might have a clean, organized locker, another's might be a mess. It depends on the person.

Instead of separate boxes, gender is more like a line or a continuum. One end of the line is masculine, the other end is feminine, and what's in between isn't completely masculine or feminine, but a little of both. That's where most of us are, somewhere in between.

Each person is different. That's one of the great things about being human. Each of us brings different attitudes, experiences, and strengths into the mix. If we were all alike—or if all boys were alike and all girls were alike—the world would be as boring as having plain white bread for breakfast, lunch, and dinner every day.

Even though gender roles can sometimes help you make sense of the world, they can also limit your potential to be the best you can be and to freely add your own unique personality and experiences to all that you do. Gender roles can make you feel that if you're not acting a certain way—if you're a boy who doesn't like sports or a girl who doesn't like to go shopping—then something's wrong with you. They can make you think you're not good enough just as you are. They can cause you to judge other people. You can't be at your best when you're judging yourself or others in these ways.

Different but equal

Despite having a lot in common, girls and boys *are* different in some ways. Because of these differences, there are people who have concluded that one sex must be better than the other. As one girl wrote in her survey, "Everyone's equal no matter what, but some people in our society choose to rank people lower than what they should be." When people start to think this way, it's easy to decide that one sex should get more respect, more rights, or better opportunities. But the fact that the sexes are different doesn't mean one is better than the other. Another teen summed this up by saying, "Just because we were made different doesn't mean we should be treated different."

THE SURVEY SAID:

80% of girls think girls and boys are equal.
74% of boys think boys and girls are equal.

So, does boy = girl? No, that doesn't make sense. But here are some other formulas that do:

expectations for boys = expectations for girls

value of boys = value of girls

opportunities for girls = opportunities for boys

rights of boys = rights of girls

treatment of girls = treatment of boys

The best way to express this might be to say that the two sexes are different, but equal. And that's what makes life interesting!

"It's very simple: girl = human, boy = human, human = human."
Boy, 13

Find out more!

Changing Bodies, Changing Lives by Ruth Bell and other coauthors of *Our Bodies, Ourselves* and *Ourselves and Our Children,* with members of the Teen Book Project (New York: Times Books, 1998). This book is full of information about all the changes that come with puberty, and includes lots of quotes by teenagers who have been through it.

Straight Talk About Anger by Christine Dentemaro and Rachel Kranz (New York: Facts On File, 1995). This comprehensive book offers sound advice about dealing with anger—yours and other people's. It includes information about what causes anger and suggestions for coping with it in healthy ways.

The What's Happening to My Body? Book for Boys by Lynda Madaras (New York: Newmarket Press, 2000). This updated edition has tons of information on boys' bodies, sexuality, emotions, and puberty. And check out the companion quiz book and journal by the same author: *My Body, My Self for Boys* (New York: Newmarket Press, 2000).

The What's Happening to My Body? Book for Girls by Lynda Madaras (New York: Newmarket Press, 2000). This updated classic covers everything you want to know about body changes, feelings, sexuality, menstruation, and more. Also look for *My Feelings, My Self: A Growing-Up Journal for Girls* (New York: Newmarket Press, 2002).

Neuroscience for Kids
faculty.washington.edu/chudler/neurok.html
If you're interested in research on the brain, visit this Web site. Sign up for the online newsletter, enter the writing contest, send "brainy" e-postcards, or check out the site's fun experiments and activities. You'll also find books, magazines, and links to more information about the brain. To find research on "She Brains-He Brains," go to *faculty.washington.edu/chudler/heshe.html.*

Warning Signs
helping.apa.org/warningsigns
This is the American Psychological Association's Web site on violence prevention for teens. Click on "Dealing with anger" for some helpful ways to cope with angry feelings.

Gender traits?

☐ INDEPENDENT ___   ☐ LOGICAL ___   ☐ *conceited* ___

☐ **helpful** ___   ☐ *leader* ___   ☐ **likable** ___

☐ *cheerful* ___   ☐ **truthful** ___   ☐ quiet ___

☐ **OUTSPOKEN** ___   ☐ **messy** ___   ☐ **SERIOUS** ___

☐ **MOODY** ___   ☐ forgiving ___   ☐ CONTROLLING ___

☐ shy ___   ☐ **kind** ___   ☐ *easily hurt* ___

☐ ATHLETIC ___   ☐ *sensitive* ___   ☐ **gentle** ___

☐ **loving** ___   ☐ *risk taker* ___   ☐ **trusting** ___

☐ SELF-CONFIDENT ___   ☐ peacemaker ___   ☐ *lazy* ___

☐ needy ___   ☐ COMPETITIVE ___   ☐ troublemaker ___

☐ good listener ___   ☐ emotional ___   ☐ **assertive** ___

Chapter 3

GROWING UP BOY, GROWING UP GIRL

SURVEY COMMENTS:
Do teens think parents treat boys and girls equally?

"Maybe. I've never seen it happen, though." —Girl, 13   "Yes, and they should." —Boy, 14

"No! My parents treat my brother with so much more liberty than me. They say that girls and guys have to be raised differently! Unfair!" —Girl, 14

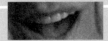

"No, but they may not always know they're being unfair." —Boy, 12

"Yes—why would they treat one better than the other?" —Girl, 12

"In my culture, some families honor boys more." —Boy, 15

"I don't know. It depends on where the parent was raised. Like if girls were considered higher than boys or if girls were supposed to obey all males." —Girl, 14

"My mom treats boys better than she treats girls. My dad treats everyone equal all of the time." —Girl, 12

"Mothers usually favor daughters. Fathers usually favor sons." —Boy, 14

"My parents will sometimes brag about my brother and won't even talk about me." —Girl, 11

"Parents are sometimes more lenient towards girls." —Boy, 13

"Parents seem to give males more privileges as well as more respect." —Girl, 15

"In a household it's a parent's obligation that both genders are treated fairly." —Boy, 13

"When a little boy falls and scrapes his knee, the mother is like, 'You're a big boy, go and play,' but if it's a girl they say, 'Oh, poor little girl, let's put a bandage on it.'" —Boy, 16

Equal treatment at home?

From the day you joined your family, the people you lived with have sent you messages about what they expect from you because you're a girl or a boy. Your family—and especially your parents—were the first people to teach you about gender and gender roles. Through the years, the ways they've acted and the things they've said have influenced your ideas about what it means to be female or male.

A word about families

Families come in many forms. When we use the word parents, we're talking about the adult or adults at home who are responsible for you. And when we say sisters or brothers, we're talking about other kids who live with you. Even if the people you live with aren't actually related to you, they're still your family.

THE SURVEY SAID:

36% of girls said parents and teachers treat girls and boys equally.
22% of girls said parents and teachers sometimes treat girls and boys equally.
39% of girls said parents and teachers do not treat girls and boys equally.
38% of boys said parents and teachers treat boys and girls equally.
15% of boys said parents and teachers sometimes treat boys and girls equally.
44% of boys said parents and teachers do not treat boys and girls equally.

(These percentages don't add up to 100% because some people didn't answer or wrote "N/A.")

Growing up, you probably noticed that parents expected different things from girls and boys. In our survey, we asked whether parents (and teachers—discussed in Chapter 4) treated boys and girls equally. People's answers were really mixed, but they showed that teens of both sexes felt things were *not* equal a good deal of the time.

WHAT DO YOU THINK?

* Do you think parents treat girls and boys equally? What's it like in your family? In your friends' families?

* Do you think parents should always treat girls and boys the same? Why or why not?

Remember when?

One of the earliest lessons your parents or other caregivers taught you about gender probably began with the toys they gave you to play with. Maybe you've heard the expression "Play is the work of children." It means that play is children's job—it teaches them about things they'll do when they grow up. For instance, playing with a toy workbench teaches about tools and fixing things. Playing with a baby doll teaches about caring for a baby. Now, it's been a while, and you may not spend much time with dolls or toy trucks these days—but try to remember what it was like when you did. As you grew, the toys your parents gave you to play with and the activities they urged you to do may have sent messages about gender roles. If you played with that workbench, you got to feel the power of pounding wood with a hammer. If you had a doll to dress and feed, you got to learn how important it is to take care of other people.

GENDER FACT

One study of preschoolers (children three, four, and five years old) showed how adults can subtly send messages about gender roles when it comes to toys. In the study, when boys asked their parents to buy them action figures, the adults would buy these toys 70% of the time. When boys asked parents to buy fashion dolls, the adults would buy the dolls 40% of the time. This means that parents were making a judgment about which type of doll was more appropriate for boys. Some of the boys were learning that an action figure is a more acceptable toy for a boy than a fashion doll is.

Other kids may have influenced what you played with, too. Child-development experts say that usually by the time kids are about six years old, they see gender rules as being set. They've figured out that certain toys must be meant for girls (dolls, fancy dress-up clothes, tea-party sets, miniature stoves), and certain toys must be meant for boys (trucks, racing cars, bulldozers, toy guns). In many children's

eyes, if you play with the wrong thing you're breaking the rules. Children often make fun of boys for playing with "girl toys" or girls for playing with "boy toys." No one likes to get picked on, so kids will often just play with something they think is more acceptable just to avoid being teased. Boys are really treated unfairly here. A girl is less likely to get made fun of for playing with a truck than a boy is for playing with a doll or a kitchen set. That means that early on boys get less of a chance than girls to learn about things like taking care of children or cooking.

Parents sometimes label activities as "boy things" and "girl things," too. Boys and girls both grow up swimming or playing soccer or T-ball, but there are certain sports and activities that are considered for boys and others for girls. Baseball, hockey, and football are often mostly for boys, while softball, figure skating, gymnastics, and ballet or tap dancing are mostly for girls. Sure, there are girls who play hockey (or want to) and boys who like (or want) to dance, but many times parents and other kids make it clear that they think it's weird for a girl to like rough sports or for a boy to enjoy more artistic activities like gymnastics or ballet.

What's the point of talking about toys you no longer play with and activities you may no longer do? Looking back gives you a picture of how your ideas about gender started forming. It gives you clues about yourself—and about your parents and other people in your family, too.

WHAT DO YOU THINK?

* Why do you think kids sometimes tease other kids for playing with the "wrong" toy for their sex?

* What were your favorite toys when you were little? Your favorite pastimes? Why did you like them? Were they considered "girl" or "boy" things, or were they for anybody?

* Which toys and activities didn't you like as much? Why?

* If you're a girl who liked some "boy things" or a boy who liked some "girl things," how did your parents react? How about the other people in your family? Your friends? Did they support you? Tease you?

* Are there things you *didn't* do as a child that you now wish you had done? Do these things have anything to do with gender?

Roles in the family

Roles are just the names for the different kinds of things that we do in our lives. Each person in a family has lots of roles. For example, consider a made-up two-parent family: Carlos and Julia Garcia and their children Penelope and Tony:

Mrs. Garcia is married to Mr. Garcia, so she's a wife. She was married and divorced before, so she's also an ex-wife. She has two children (one from her first marriage and one with Mr. Garcia), so she's a mom, too. Mrs. Garcia is a daughter as well, and her parents live nearby. When people in the family are sick or hurt, Mrs. Garcia comforts and cares for them. She's also strict, and if Penelope or Tony get a low grade or start fighting, they know their mom will discipline them. At home, Mrs. Garcia cooks many of the meals (her husband cooks some, too); handles the family budget; washes clothes for herself, her husband, and Tony; and does a lot of the cleaning. Away from home, Mrs. Garcia works at an auto-parts plant and does volunteer work at school and at the local community center. If we made a chart to show some of Mrs. Garcia's roles, it might look like this:

Mrs. Garcia

family roles: mom, wife, ex-wife, daughter

ways of relating at home: caregiver, disciplinarian

jobs at home: cook, banker, clothes washer, cleaner

jobs and interests outside the home: factory worker, volunteer, friend

Charts for the rest of the Garcia family might look like these:

Mr. Garcia

family roles: stepfather, father, husband, son-in-law

ways of relating at home: listener, peacemaker

jobs at home: mechanic, homework helper, cook, vacuumer

jobs and interests outside the home: police officer, singer, friend

Penelope Garcia, 14

family roles: daughter, stepdaughter, half sister

ways of relating at home: helper, mischief maker

jobs at home: sitter, vacuumer, clothes washer, dog walker

jobs and interests outside the home: student, pianist, basketball player, baby-sitter, friend

Tony Garcia, 8

family roles: son, half brother

ways of relating at home: problem solver, jokester

jobs at home: dishwasher, dog-walker, recycler

jobs and interests outside the home: student, soccer player, miniature car collector, friend

Like the members of the Garcia family, each of us has some kind of a family role, and many people have more than one. We all have ways we relate to other people in our family. We all have jobs we do at home. And we all have things we do away from home.

WHAT DO YOU THINK?

* If you made a chart for people in your family, what would their roles be?

* What are your roles at home?

Often roles and jobs in the family have something to do with gender. In fact, sometimes gender roles for parents end up looking something like this chart from prehistoric times.

Parent roles in prehistoric times

MEN	WOMEN
• Go off hunting for food	• Gather nearby plants for food
• Protect family from predators	• Have and care for babies
• Make and use tools	• Prepare and serve food

In some two-parent families, moms and dads have responsibilities and do things that seem typically masculine or feminine: moms cook, clean, do laundry, and care for children while dads have a job outside the home, do the heavy chores, discipline the kids, and handle the finances. In other families, moms and dads divide these things up differently—some things may seem to be based on typical gender roles, while others don't. In families with a single parent, the adult might play a lot more roles, or the kids might have more responsibilities—maybe based on gender, maybe not. The roles in every family are a little different.

For years, many families consisted of a dad who went to a job to make money and a mom who stayed home and watched the kids and took care of the home. Even for families that weren't set up this way, the image we got from TV, magazines, and advertising showed this family. (For more about how the media and popular culture affect gender roles, see Chapter 6.) Just like with lots of other things, society had decided that different things were acceptable for moms to do and for dads to do. Typical jobs for moms were caretaking and teaching—from changing diapers, to comforting a sick or hurt child, to reading stories, to feeding the family. Jobs for dads often included things like going off to work to earn money, disciplining the kids, and playing sports or physical games with them.

That's not the way it is for many people anymore. Yet there's still a strong idea in society that moms do the housework and take care of the kids (whether or not they work outside the home) and dads come home from work and toss a ball around outside with the boys or make grilled-cheese sandwiches as a favor to Mom. These strong ideas can make it hard for people to figure out how to work together as a family.

GENDER FACTS

According to the 2000 U.S. Census:

* 9.8 million of single-parent families are headed by women; 2.1 million are headed by men.

* Single-parent families account for about 27% of all families with children.

* In most two-parent households, both of the adults work outside the home.

The family scene: Chores

One of the areas where families need to work together is chores, and families often assign chores differently for boys than for girls. Figuring out chores based on a person's sex is another kind of gender stereotype.

THE SURVEY ASKED:

At home, are chores the same for girls and boys?

GIRLS SAID:

"I know my mom thinks boys shouldn't have to clean as much as girls."

"Boys get more masculine jobs, like fixing things, but girls get cleaning bathrooms."

"The chores are not the same, because the boys always get less, and easier ones."

"I mow the lawn, my brother does the clothes, I paint the garage, and the other way around."

"Sometimes my mom makes me do housework and my brother has to help my dad. I like to help my dad and I hate housework."

"My parents make the girls cook and do most of the cleaning. I don't think that's fair because my brother is ten years old, and when I was his age I already knew how to cook, but my brother doesn't."

"I think that parents have higher expectations of guys and have them work harder. Like recently my dad had my brothers help him chop down a tree but he wouldn't let me help because it wasn't safe."

BOYS SAID:

"Boys do more physical chores like shoveling and lawn mowing."

"Me and my brother always get the dirty work and my sister gets the laundry."

"Men have to do all the hard jobs while women stay home and clean."

"Taking out the trash and cleaning your room applies to everyone in my home."

"In my house we do all the chores together."

"Boys have to do chores like fixing things around the house, and the girls' chores are more centered—NO OFFENSE—around the kitchen."

"My sister doesn't have to do chores for allowance, but I do."

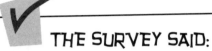

THE SURVEY SAID:

**34% of boys said they thought boys and girls have to do similar chores
and follow the same rules at home. (For more about rules, see pages 44–50.)**

6% of boys said that sometimes chores and rules were the same for both sexes.

45% of boys said they thought chores and rules were different for boys than for girls.

**37% of girls said they thought girls and boys have to do similar chores
and follow the same rules at home.**

9% of girls said that sometimes chores and rules were the same for both sexes.

43% of girls said they thought chores and rules were different for girls than for boys.

(These percentages don't add up to 100% because some people didn't answer or wrote "N/A.")

In our survey, a lot of the boys felt that they got saddled with the hard chores while the girls got to do easier ones. And a lot of the girls felt like *they* got stuck with the hard jobs while the boys got off easy. These people might all have a point. It's true that many of the chores boys end up doing are physically harder. It's also true that many of these chores only need to be done once in a while. Typical "girls' chores" usually aren't as physically strenuous, but they often need to be done on a more regular basis. Having something to eat and clean clothes to wear are things that need to happen all the time. This means girls sometimes end up spending more time every day doing their chores.

Most people don't like chores, but they're necessary. Doing chores based on gender stereotypes (such as boys taking out the garbage or washing the car while girls do dishes or clean the bathroom) can keep you from learning. Face it, everyone will have to know how to do a load of laundry, cook a meal, or fix a leaky faucet. Even if you're happy with the way chores are divided up in your home, take a chance and try someone else's jobs once in a while. You and your family might appreciate the change, and you could learn something new about yourself (like maybe you actually have a knack for plumbing!).

One way to see how fairly chores are being divided is by keeping a chore chart. Photocopy the chart on page 53. Fill it in over the next week, noting who does each chore (it might be more than one person) and how long it takes. Rank how hard the chore is using E for easy, M for medium, H for hard, and S for strenuous. When the week is over, total the hours each person spends on home chores. Who spends the most time? The least? Who does the more physically demanding work? Are the chores divided up along gender lines?

With your chore chart in hand, you can take the first step toward making things more fair in your family. If you think the idea of switching chores around will go over pretty well, set up a family meeting. Show what you found using the chore chart, and talk about ways to make the chores more fair for everyone in the family, male and female. If you think it will be hard to convince people to change, you might try a different approach and just offer to do a chore that someone else usually does.

6 tips for making chores gender-fair and hassle-free

Is your family having trouble figuring out how to make the chores work better for everyone? Here are a few ideas.

1. **Work together.** Things go faster if you do them together. For example, cook meals together, or have one person cook while the other sets the table. Try a dishwashing assembly line where one person clears the dishes and wipes the table and counters, another washes, and another dries. If people's schedules are too busy to use the group-chore approach every night, try it once a week for a while.

2. **Choose favorite chores.** Some people like dusting and vacuuming better than mopping the floor—other people have different ideas. So make a list of household chores and have people choose what they want to do. And for those chores nobody likes much (or the ones people fight over, like walking the dog), take turns. Just be sure to keep track of whose turn it is.

3. **Offer to help.** If you're sitting around and your brother or sister is busy working on something, ask if you can lend a hand. If your mom or dad always does the laundry but has been too busy lately to get to it, come to the rescue. It's better than wearing dirty clothes, and in the future Dad or Mom will probably remember what you did and return the favor.

4. **Ask for help.** If you feel like you're doing more than your fair share, or if you have too much to do and can't get it all done, ask someone to pitch in.

5. **Be flexible.** Life is always changing, so try not to get into rigid chore patterns. Be open to learning new things, too. It can be hard to try something that you've always assumed was another person's job. But, hey, learning something new can make you a smarter, more independent person.

6. **Say thanks.** You know how good it feels when people notice something you've done. Do the same for them. If a meal was good, speak up. If you're glad to have clean clothes, say so.

The family scene: Rules

For most teens, rules at home can be a real hot-button issue. There are rules about curfews, homework, how you dress, and how much time you spend

on the phone or computer or watching TV. Sometimes the rules feel like they're just there to make your life difficult. Parents usually say they set rules because they want what's best for you (which may be true), but that can be hard to believe, especially when the rules seem unfair.

In our survey, a lot of people felt that rules at home *aren't* always fair. When it came to rules and gender roles, only about one-third of both boys and girls thought that parents set the same rules for kids regardless of sex. That means that most of the people we surveyed think that boys and girls end up with two different sets of rules some or most of the time. (The survey statistics about this are on page 42.)

THE SURVEY ASKED:

At home, are rules about things like clothes, curfews, or talking on the phone the same for boys and for girls? Are boys and girls disciplined for the same things and in the same ways?

BOYS SAID:

"My sister gets to do more stuff, like go out with her friends and talk on the phone longer. She also gets more privacy."

"Most girls' rules are stricter. I think this is because parents think too much freedom will lead to sex and pregnancy."

"I think we boys have more freedom and get more responsibility."

"Girls are expected to follow the rules and be more responsible."

"Girls always get what they want."

"My sisters never get disciplined for fighting, but I do."

GIRLS SAID:

"When I get restrictions it's from the phone and my brother is from the computer."

"Some parents (subconsciously) let their sons have later curfews or date earlier than their daughters."

"I think in some cases the boy may get more freedom because he's strong and can protect himself if needed."

"Boys aren't disciplined as hard as girls are because they'll say, 'Oh, he's a boy, so it's okay, but a girl isn't supposed to do that.'"

"Boys are disciplined harsher."

"My parents weren't as strict with my brother as they are with me."

WHAT DO YOU THINK?

✴ If you're a girl with a brother or a boy with a sister, do you feel the rules are different or similar? In what ways?

✴ If you don't have a sibling, do you feel any of the rules you have to follow are based on whether you're a girl or a boy? Why do you think that?

✴ Does it ever make sense to have different family rules for boys or girls? If it does, when? Why? If it doesn't, why not?

Teens who took the survey pointed out that rules can be different based on a number of things, including:

✴ **Age.** A lot of people who answered our survey said that kids in the family had different rules, but that these rules were based on how old they were. As kids get older and show that they're able to accept more responsibility, parents are more willing to give more freedom.

✴ **Personal needs.** Sometimes different rules may seem unfair, but are really based on who you are as an individual. If you're having trouble with your grades but your brother or sister isn't, you may have rules about no TV before your homework is done, while he or she doesn't. Your parents may think you're the only one who needs that rule.

✴ **Safety.** Often, parents tend to be stricter with their daughters because they worry about their safety. Many teens talked about this

on their surveys. "Girls always have to have their parents see their boyfriend before they go on a date," wrote one girl, "but boys don't." A boy told us, "I think parents are more protective of girls." Parents may feel that girls, who are generally smaller than boys and not as strong, can be taken advantage of sexually or physically harmed. But if parents worry that girls aren't safe from boys, shouldn't they be worrying about what they're teaching boys about how to treat girls? And if a parent thinks a situation isn't safe enough for their daughter, how can she or he assume it's safe for a boy? Some girls are more capable of defending themselves than some boys. Sadly, both girls *and* boys are at risk. And both boys and girls are capable of making wise or not-so-wise choices, and of choosing to harm people or treat them with respect. We'll talk more about safety in Chapter 7, pages 145–146.

WHAT DO YOU THINK?

* If you want a rule changed, how can you show your dad or mom that you're ready to handle the responsibility?

* Do you think it's fair when sisters and brothers have different rules? Why or why not? When is it fair? When isn't it?

* What kind of safety issues exist for girls? For boys?

* If girls aren't as safe as boys are, what can boys and girls do to improve this situation?

* If boys and men sometimes harm girls, what can girls and boys do about it?

Unwritten rules

Most family rules aren't actually written down in some notebook where you can turn to a certain page and show, for example, the rules for using the phone. Usually, though, families do have certain clear rules that have been talked about openly (even if not everybody likes them). But there are some rules for girls and boys that families don't necessarily talk about, yet somehow people know what these rules are. These are called unwritten rules.

Based on our survey, if you wrote down some of those unwritten rules that often exist for girls and boys, they might look like these:

Unwritten rules

GIRLS	BOYS
• Be a good girl!	• Boys will be boys.
• If you can't say something nice, don't say anything at all.	• Don't start fights, but stick up for yourself if you have to.
• Girls don't roughhouse.	• Don't show your feelings.
• It's okay to be weak.	• Boys don't cry.
• Act like a lady.	• Be strong.
• Girls need protecting.	• Boys can take care of themselves.

There were plenty of girls in the survey who felt they had to act "sweet," "perfect," or "well behaved." Even more noticeable were the boys who wrote about having to be "tough," "manly," or "macho." One boy wrote, "I hate it when something happens that hurts me and I wimp out or cry." Another boy said, "My dad always calls me a wussy when I cry." (For more on labels like "wussy," "sissy," and "butch," see pages 90–92.)

Boys who feel like they always have to act tough and never show their emotions are under a lot of strain. So are girls who feel like they have to be sweet and pleasant all the time. Adults will sometimes say things like, "Be a man," or "That wasn't very lady-like." Those words can really hurt, and they send a powerful message about what's appropriate behavior for girls and boys. Even worse, sometimes people get punished for breaking the unwritten rules.

In the surveys, there were people who brought up manners as well. Some girls felt like if they accidentally belched, they'd be picked up by the manners police. One girl said, "They expect us girls not to put our elbows on the table, not to burp, to always wipe our hands and mouth. I know we should be polite, but shouldn't the boys, also?" Several boys told us that they felt not only excused from good manners, but that it was *expected* that they'd burp and make rude noises—that this was "normal" for boys. These are gender stereotypes for sure!

WHAT DO YOU THINK?

* What are some of the unwritten rules in your family?

* What unwritten rules apply specifically to girls or to boys? How do you feel about them?

It takes a lot of courage to be yourself sometimes, but trying to be somebody else to make other people happy can be even harder. There's an old saying that rules are meant to be broken—and when it comes to unwritten rules, it's often true. It's really important for you to think about these rules and decide for yourself whether they're true and which rules you want to live by.

In most families, at least some of the rules can be negotiated. This doesn't mean your parents are going to agree with you about any rule you want to change. But if you feel pressured by family rules, or if you're unhappy with certain ones or think you're being treated unfairly, then maybe it's time you discussed this. Here are some things you might say to get the ball rolling:

"Mom, why is it that you don't want me to call guys on the phone?"

"I'd like to talk to you about my curfew. It doesn't seem fair that I can't stay out till eleven like Bob did when he was my age."

"Dad, it seems like if I come home late, I get in a lot more trouble than Jemma does when she's late."

"When I hurt my leg, I felt like you were ashamed that I cried. It hurt a lot, plus I felt really bad that you didn't think I should be crying."

It might help if you wrote down why you think a rule is unfair along with some ideas for what you think a better rule would be. If you believe the rules are based on your sex, rather than on who you are, be ready to explain why you feel that way.

Whatever your situation, be open to what the other people in your family have to say, and be willing to compromise and be flexible. You've heard it before, and it's usually true: parents are more likely to listen and loosen rules if they see that you're willing to take more responsibility and to talk things through in a mature, reasonable way.

What if you can't talk to your parents?

If you believe you can't talk to your parents about rules or other important things at home, find another adult you trust to help you. This might be

• an aunt or an uncle

• a friend's parent or another grown-up you feel comfortable with

• a teacher at school

• a leader at your place of worship

• a trained professional such as a counselor, doctor, or social worker

If you can't find an adult but need help right now:

• look in the Yellow Pages under Crisis Intervention for a local phone number to call, **OR**

• call the toll-free National Youth Crisis Hotline at **1-800-448-4663**

Where do family gender roles come from?

Whatever expectations your parents had or have about gender roles, they formed these based on their own feelings, their life experiences, the ideas of people around them, and the traditions they were raised in. And just as it's helpful for boys and girls to understand each other, knowing something about why your parents feel as they do can help you figure out how to talk to them about gender issues in your family. Here are a few conversation starters:

✦ What was it like being a girl (or a boy) when you were my age?

✦ What do you like most about being a man (or a woman)?

✦ What would you change about being a woman (or a man)?

✦ What do you want me to know about being a man (or a woman)?

Intentionally or not, your parents and other important adults in your life have taught you a lot about what it means to be male or female. Intentionally or not, you've taken many of these messages to heart. You may have learned things that make you proud and pleased to be the sex you are. You may also have learned things that make it hard for you. To help sort this out a little more, photocopy "My female family tree" and "My male family tree" (pages 54 and 55). Fill out both forms (make extra copies if you want to write about more than four adults). A regular family tree shows how all the people in your family are related. The male and female trees are different: they help you figure out who the adults are who've had the most influence in your life, what they've shown you about gender roles, and how you feel about the messages they've sent you. Keep in mind that you don't actually have to be related for someone to feel like family to you.

If you think that your male and female family trees have helped you understand yourself or the adults in your life better, you might want to share them. Maybe something on these trees made you feel really proud of someone in your family—if so, the person will probably be glad to know it. And if something on the trees upset you, take some time to write or talk with someone about it, so you can come up with ideas for how to change what bothers you or make different choices.

WHAT DO YOU THINK?

* In your family, what messages about gender roles do you agree with? Why?

* What messages don't you agree with? Why?

* What, if anything, surprised you the most about what your parents believe about women and men?

* Is there a man in your family you especially admire? What do you admire about him?

* Is there a woman in your family you especially admire? What do you admire about her?

When it comes to gender roles and gender stereotypes, *you* are the one who can start making a difference. Yes, you're still part of your family. You still have to follow rules and figure out how to get along with your parents, sisters, and brothers. But that doesn't mean you can't make choices about how you want to be as a boy or a girl. Ultimately, you are the person who's in charge of your life.

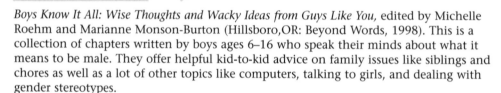

"It is each person's choice how to think and act." Boy, 15

Find out more!

Boys Know It All: Wise Thoughts and Wacky Ideas from Guys Like You, edited by Michelle Roehm and Marianne Monson-Burton (Hillsboro,OR: Beyond Words, 1998). This is a collection of chapters written by boys ages 6–16 who speak their minds about what it means to be male. They offer helpful kid-to-kid advice on family issues like siblings and chores as well as a lot of other topics like computers, talking to girls, and dealing with gender stereotypes.

Bringing Up Parents: The Teenager's Handbook by Alex J. Packer, Ph.D. (Minneapolis: Free Spirit Publishing, 1993). Here's a really funny, useful book that can help you figure out how to talk with your parents, get along better, and earn the freedom you want.

Cool Communication: A Mother and Daughter Reveal the Keys to Mutual Understanding Between Parents and Kids by Andrea Frank Henkart and Journey Henkart (New York: Penguin Putnam, 1998). This book presents honest talk from both a parent's and a teen's perspective on coping with everything from curfews to responsibility. The authors offer lots of ideas on how you can gain more trust, understanding, and respect at home.

Girl Power in the Family: A Book About Girls, Their Rights, and Their Voice by Karen Lound (Minneapolis: Lerner Publishing Group, 2000). The author of this book shares what a variety of girls have to say about growing up female in different families, explores gender roles of today and yesterday, and talks about expectations, biases, and relationships.

TeensHealth
kidshealth.org/teen
This is a health-related Web site with many articles focused on getting along with parents. Click on "Your Mind" to find "Talking to Your Parents—or Other Adults," "Why Do I Fight with My Parents So Much?" and more.

Family chore chart

Chore	Who mainly does it?	How physically hard is it? (Easy, Medium, Hard, or Strenuous)	How much time does it take per week?	Is it gender-fair?
Fix meals				
Set table				
Clear table after meals				
Wash dishes or load dishwasher				
Put away clean dishes				
Make lunches				
Take out garbage				
Put out recycling				
Make beds				
Vacuum				
Dust				
Clean bathroom(s)				
Wash clothes				
Iron clothes				
Pick up clutter				
Do outdoor work				
Care for pets				
Shop for groceries				
Other				

From *Boy v. Girl? How Gender Shapes Who We Are, What We Want, and How We Get Along* by George Abrahams, Ph.D., and Sheila Ahlbrand, copyright © 2002. Free Spirit Publishing Inc., Minneapolis, MN; 800/735-7323; www.freespirit.com. This page may be photocopied for individual, classroom, or small group work only.

My female family tree

Name:_____ Relationship:_____

Taught me this about girls/women: _____

_____

Taught me this about boys/men:_____

_____

What I think about this: _____

_____

Name:_____ Relationship:_____

Taught me this about girls/women: _____

_____

Taught me this about boys/men:_____

_____

What I think about this: _____

_____

Name:_____ Relationship:_____

Taught me this about girls/women: _____

_____

Taught me this about boys/men:_____

_____

What I think about this: _____

_____

Name:_____ Relationship:_____

Taught me this about girls/women: _____

_____

Taught me this about boys/men:_____

_____

What I think about this: _____

My male family tree

Name:_____ Relationship:_____

Taught me this about boys/men:_____

_____

Taught me this about girls/women:_____

_____

What I think about this:_____

_____

Name:_____ Relationship:_____

Taught me this about boys/men:_____

_____

Taught me this about girls/women:_____

_____

What I think about this:_____

_____

Name:_____ Relationship:_____

Taught me this about boys/men:_____

_____

Taught me this about girls/women:_____

_____

What I think about this:_____

_____

Name:_____ Relationship:_____

Taught me this about boys/men:_____

_____

Taught me this about girls/women:_____

_____

What I think about this:_____

_____

Chapter 4

MAKING THE GRADE: GENDER ISSUES IN THE CLASSROOM

SURVEY COMMENTS:

Do teens think teachers treat girls and boys equally?

"Some teachers favor their own sex and pick on people of the opposite sex. That's a MAJOR thing." —Girl, 12

"Teachers tend to give girls smaller punishments." —Boy, 14

"I think teachers treat us equally." —Girl, 13

"They're smart enough to realize that we should be treated equally, and that's part of the reason why they have their position." —Boy, 15

"Boys are treated better." —Girl, 11

"The teachers at my school are prejudiced and like the girls." —Boy, 12

"I have a male teacher who says he goes a little more easy with girls than he does with boys." —Girl, 14

"There are some teachers who treat girls with more respect. They never treat boys better than girls because they assume we are troublemakers." —Boy, 14

"Teachers always let girls go to the bathroom. They never let boys go." —Boy, 14

"Girls can get away with murder if they just smile sweetly." —Girl, 13

"Almost all teachers treat girls better. If they get in trouble nothing happens to them, just a warning. But if boys get in trouble, they send us out of the room or to in-school suspension." —Boy, 16

"In my history class, there are these guys who always goof off, and my teacher thinks it's funny. But I know if a girl did the same stuff, he'd be mad." —Girl, 15

"I think teachers offer different opportunities to boys and to girls." —Girl, 15

"Teachers have to treat everyone equal—it's part of their job." —Boy, 13

Are teachers fair to students of both sexes?

Society and family play a part in gender roles. What about school? School is supposed to be a place where girls and boys gain knowledge and learn to be confident and capable. If any institution should treat boys and girls equally, you'd think school would be that place. Is it?

In our survey, we asked if students thought teachers and parents treated the sexes equally. Out of almost 2,000 surveys, more than 800 girls and boys—40 percent—thought they did not. (You'll find the exact statistics in Chapter 3 on page 34.)

Besides asking about equal treatment, we asked this question: Do authority figures at school expect the same behavior from both boys and girls? Here again, students had mixed feelings. Many students, including a number of those who answered yes, wrote comments and examples of situations where the expectations didn't seem fair. In general, both girls and boys thought teachers and other authority figures at school expected boys to act up more and girls to be quiet and better behaved in class. A lot of teens also felt that adults were harder on boys when they got in trouble than they were on girls. Some boys especially felt that this was very unfair.

THE SURVEY ASKED:

Do authority figures at school expect the same behavior from both girls and boys?

GIRLS SAID:

"No, because they know guys are more immature."

"Most teachers expect girls to behave better than boys."

"Teachers are more lenient with boys being loud. Girls get in more trouble for talking than boys do."

"I think a lot of teachers underestimate troublemaking girls. Some authority figures do not believe a girl could get into a physical fight."

"Some teachers say girls should not act out but that it's natural for boys to do that."

"Teachers usually expect girls to be proper and stuff, while boys can be obnoxious and not get in trouble."

"Authority figures at school expect girls all to be caring and not rude and to do what they tell us."

BOYS SAID:

"I think they SHOULD."

"I think authorities expect better from girls than from boys."

"They expect boys to screw up and not follow the rules."

"They'll say, 'I'd expect more from a thirteen-year-old.' It's more about your age than gender."

"They think we boys are wild and destructive."

"They expect boys to act up and girls to act well."

"It seems like they're almost looking for me to get into trouble."

GIRLS SAID:

"They expect us both to follow the same rules."

"Guys are almost always suspected when something happens."

BOYS SAID:

"I think they're fair to both boys and girls."

"To authority figures, boys are evil."

 THE SURVEY SAID:

49% of girls said authority figures at school expect the same behavior from both girls and boys.
4% of girls said authority figures at school expect the same behavior some of the time.
37% of girls said authority figures at school don't expect the same behavior from both girls and boys.
48% of boys said authority figures at school expect the same behavior from both boys and girls.
3% of boys said authority figures at school expect the same behavior some of the time.
41% of boys said authority figures at school don't expect the same behavior from both boys and girls.

(These percentages don't add up to 100% because some people didn't answer or wrote "N/A.")

WHAT DO YOU THINK?

* Do you think teachers should always treat boys and girls the same? Why or why not?

* What are some ways teachers treat girls and boys equally? What are some ways they don't?

* Why do you think some teachers treat one sex better than the other?

* Do you feel different about classes where teachers treat boys and girls equally and have fair expectations? Where they don't? In what ways?

Some students who took the survey said they felt teachers tried to be fair. Others pointed out that girls and boys really do behave differently at times, so it's natural for teachers to have different expectations. While this may be true in some cases, it's also possible that boys and girls take on the gender roles they feel are expected of them.

Those gender stereotypes that seem to lurk everywhere are one reason for these expectations. Another reason might be the differences some scientists are finding in male and female brains. In Chapter 2 (pages 25–28), you read about some of these differences and how they affect the ways boys and girls think, learn, and act. Teachers know about this scientific research, too. And knowing about it can make it seem natural to expect boys to be more aggressive, physical, and loud and to expect girls to be more quiet, thoughtful, and willing to follow rules.

Equality at school: How far have we come?

Before we look more at those learning and behavior differences, let's take a short trip back in history. You probably know that there was a time when schools treated girls and boys *very* differently. Boys were taught that they'd grow up to be the family wage earners. Girls learned that their job would be to care for their husbands and their children. Boys took lots of math and science courses, along with industrial arts classes like machine shop and auto repair. Girls took lots of English classes along with home economics—things like sewing and family budgeting. Fifty years ago, it would have been highly unusual to see a boy in a cooking class or a girl learning woodworking.

To make things more equal, in 1972 the U.S. Congress passed a set of laws called the Educational Amendments of 1972. These laws made a lot of improvements for schools. One part of this group of laws is called Title IX, which states that males and females need to have the same rights and privileges in school.

Title IX

No person in the United States shall, on the basis of sex, be excluded from participation in, be denied the benefits of, or be subjected to discrimination under any educational program or activity receiving federal financial assistance.

Simply put, if you go to a school that gets money from the government (and most schools do), then that school has to make sure that girls and boys get treated the same way and have the same opportunities. Here are a few things the law requires publicly funded schools to do so things are fair for students of both sexes:

* Schools can't require or refuse a student's participation in any class because of the person's sex.

* Whenever a school finds that a class has a lot more students of one sex than another, the school must take action to make sure that it isn't because of a bias in counseling or testing.

* A school can't give awards or make selections on the basis of sex. For example, there can't be awards for the top male student and the top female student. There can't be three slots for girls and three slots for boys on the debating team. People have to earn these things and be selected regardless of what sex they are.

* Boys and girls have to have locker rooms, toilets, and shower facilities that are similar in quality.

Although Title IX is a law, that doesn't mean these things will always be true. Laws are constantly tested and reinterpreted. This is especially true for laws like Title IX that are controversial. As people take Title IX cases to court, lawyers and judges are arguing and deciding exactly what the law means in different situations and how this affects you.

Title IX is there to help *both* girls and boys. It deals with all kinds of things from school sports to sexual harassment (two topics discussed in Chapter 5), from how you're treated in class to the kind of courses you can sign up for. Still, for many years, most schools focused on making things fair for girls as the way to live up to Title IX requirements. Several boys in the survey remarked on this, saying it didn't seem fair. One boy wrote, "Everyone was so worried about making schools equal for girls that they started favoring them." Another commented, "Some teachers have a distorted view that all girls are being oppressed and that it's their duty to grade them better, talk to them, let them do things first, etc."

Before Title IX . . . and after

You may think that things aren't so bad that a country would actually need a law to make sure boys and girls get treated equally, but back in 1972 when the law was passed, it was pretty different. One way to measure this is by looking at professional careers of men and women:

In 1972 . . .

• men earned 93% of all law degrees, 91% of medical degrees, and 99% of dental degrees

• women earned 7% of all law degrees, 9% of medical degrees, and 1% of dental degrees

Primarily as a result of Title IX, 22 years later . . .

• men earned 57% of all law degrees and 62% of medical and dental degrees

• women earned 43% of all law degrees, 38% of medical degrees, and 38% of dental degrees

These statistics show that having equal opportunities for girls in school has made a huge difference over the years.

WHAT DO YOU THINK?

✱ Has there been so much focus on making things equal for girls that boys have been treated unfairly? If so, in what ways?

✱ How do you feel about a law that tells schools they have to treat girls and boys in the same way?

In the 1990s, several studies were done to look at how schools had changed since Title IX became law. Some of the findings match the experiences of those students in the survey who said that things still aren't fair. One study called "Beyond Title IX: Gender Equity Issues in Schools" found that while some progress had been made, there were still problems in several areas, including these:

✱ Fewer girls than boys were participating and achieving in math and science.

✱ Boys were getting more attention from teachers—praise, help, and criticism—and were being given more time to talk in class than girls.

✱ Boys were receiving harsher punishments than girls for the same offenses.

Other studies supported the findings that boys were doing better in math and science and getting more attention than girls, leaving many girls behind in the learning curve. Today, researchers are becoming more interested in the ways that boys are being treated unfairly and the kinds of problems boys as well as girls are experiencing at school.

Do you think teachers and other authority figures at your school treat girls and boys fairly? If you like, use the "Gender-friendly classroom checklist" on page 77 to look at some of the ways things are equal or not-so-equal in your school.

How is it possible that schools might treat both girls *and* boys unfairly? Some experts think the answer has to do with brain differences. If boys and girls think differently, then a way of teaching that works for boys might not work so well for girls, and the other way around. In this case, it only makes sense that there are going to be different ways that are easier for boys and girls to learn, at least in some instances.

Do the ways students learn and act in school depend on gender?

Here are some things experts have learned about how girls and boys are doing in school, how teachers interact with kids of each sex, and what kinds of expectations schools have for boys and girls.

At school

BOYS	GIRLS
• achieve test scores in math and science that are slightly higher	• achieve test scores in reading, writing, and the arts that are slightly higher
• are louder and more active in class and get more attention, but much of it is negative attention	• are quieter in class, but get less attention than boys
• receive 70% of the D's and F's	• receive 60% of the A's
• drop out of school at a slightly higher rate	• are more likely to go on to college
• constitute 80% of ADD and ADHD (attention deficit and hyperactivity) diagnoses	• are more often diagnosed as depressed
• are three times more likely to be victims of violence on school property	• are more likely to be sexually harassed
• participate more in sports music or performing arts, academic	• participate more in student council, yearbook, and school newspaper

The hormonal changes common in puberty can affect behavior. For example, changes in testosterone levels can cause many boys to respond more physically to things. This means that boys might be more restless in class, while girls may find it easier to sit calmly and answer questions. These different ways of acting often get very different responses from teachers (and other students)—which can make the experience of school different for girls and boys.

When a boy has trouble sitting still in class, the teacher has to spend more time with him than with the girl who is quietly doing her assignment. The girl can feel ignored, as if she isn't as important as the boy. But this situation isn't great for the boy either. If he's constantly being told to sit down, pay attention, and leave other people alone, he may begin to feel like school is a place where he can't do anything right.

Think about it. If your teachers have been reacting to boys and girls this way from the time you were in kindergarten, it could have had a pretty big impact on how you think about school as you move through middle school and high school.

♀ Girls' view: Girls who feel like the boys get all of the attention may quit trying to get the teacher to notice them. They might stop asking questions or raising their hand in class discussions. Even if they still do their homework and get high or passing grades, they might feel like what they have to say isn't important. Or maybe they'll start to do whatever they can to get attention, including acting up in class.

♂ Boys' view: A boy who is constantly told to settle down may start to feel like a failure. Sensing that teachers aren't on his side can lead to a bad attitude toward school and teachers. Some boys get so frustrated that they give up. Even when things aren't this extreme, all those messages to boys about their problem behaviors over the years can still be discouraging.

STEREOTYPE ALERT!

Could it really be as simple as this? Probably not! Talking about these differences gets complicated . . . it's all too easy to start to think in terms of gender stereotypes. These are generalizations, and they don't apply to all boys or all girls (or all teachers). It's tricky, because looking at the ideas can help you think about your own experience (which may be unique) and how you'd like to have things be in school, but you don't want to start thinking strictly in terms of these roles. You always have to deal with each person as an individual. For teachers, too, looking at girls and boys in these ways can be both helpful and harmful. It can be helpful for teachers to present material in ways that make learning easier. It can be harmful to simply expect rowdiness or quiet listening without getting to know individual students.

Many of the students we surveyed wrote comments about the differences between how girls and boys approach learning. Here are some of the things they said.

Teens' comments on learning in school

GIRLS SAID:	BOYS SAID:
"Girls are not supposed to be good at math."	"Girls are always organized."
"In general, boys think in broader, 'factual' aspects."	"Boys are better at computers."
"Boys are more rowdy in class and in the hallways and seem to answer more questions in class. It seems like most girls are pressured to not answer questions as often."	"Girls are more methodical and think about more than one thing at a time. Guys are spur-of-the-moment thinkers, and think about one thing at a time."
"For a girl, good grades mean you're a nerd."	"We think differently about different subjects."
"Girls are smarter than boys."	"In middle school, girls are smarter, but in high school boys are."
"I know smart girls and smart boys."	"Boys usually choose action over words."
"I think girls tend to think outside the box more of the time."	"Boys think differently—it's scientifically proven."

Whatever your general way of learning and acting in class, there are a couple of strategies that might help you feel more confident.

If you're a hands-on, energetic, physical learner:

* **Talk to your teacher.** Ask if there are more active or hands-on activities or other study approaches that could help you learn better.

❋ **Find ways to channel your energy.** Maybe you think better when you're moving. If so, bring a stress releaser (you know, one of those little spongy things you can fit in your hand and squeeze) to class and squeeze it when you feel yourself getting frustrated or when you're working on an assignment. Make sure you get plenty of exercise to help you focus and be calmer when you need to.

❋ **Give everyone a turn.** If you're quick to raise your hand, make it a point to wait a beat before you answer a question. First, take a quick look around you to see if anyone else may want to answer it.

❋ **Ask for time.** Maybe you know the answer or idea, but can't quite think of how to express it. Tell your teacher, "I really think I know this, but I have to figure out how to explain it. Can you give me a couple of minutes to think it through?"

If you're a quieter learner who prefers to watch and listen:

❋ **Ask questions.** It can be intimidating to speak up, especially in a large group. But if you have a question and don't ask it, you miss an opportunity to learn something you didn't know before. Other people might have the same question, too, and be too shy to ask—so make the move yourself!

❋ **Ask to work in small groups.** Being with a few other students can prod you to get more actively involved and can help you start to feel more comfortable speaking and interacting.

❋ **Don't be afraid to look smart.** If you know the answer, raise your hand. Coming up with the right answer to a difficult question can be a real confidence booster. If you're good at a certain subject, it's okay to show it. You may be able to help someone who's having trouble. Then maybe that person can help *you* with something at another time.

Of course, everyone needs to eat healthy food, drink plenty of liquids, and get at least eight hours of sleep each night. It's hard to concentrate when you're hungry, dehydrated, or tired. Do your best not to skip meals. Pack a quick snack (easy on the sugar!). Bring a bottle of water to school and make sure to drink often.

Separate but equal?

There are some people who think that boys and girls will be treated more fairly in school and have the best chance at a good education if the two sexes are separated. You, or someone you know, might go to an all-girls or an all-boys school. For a long time, teachers, parents, and students have debated the pros and cons of separate-sex schools.

Arguments for separating girls and boys:

* **The other sex can be distracting.** Instead of listening to the teacher, have you ever found yourself looking at that certain girl or boy in the front row and wondering if you should try talking to the person after class?

* **The other sex can be intimidating.** At one time or another, you've probably been in a class where all the girls or all the boys seemed to understand exactly what was going on, but you felt really lost and confused. Maybe you were afraid to ask questions because you didn't want anyone to know you weren't catching on to something that they seemed to think was so obvious.

* **The other sex studies differently.** Have you ever been in a class where the girls were sitting still and reading and you couldn't concentrate because it was too quiet? Or where the boys were talking loudly and moving around and you couldn't think because it was too noisy?

Even though the traits and behaviors thought to be typical of boys or girls don't always apply *just* to boys or *just* to girls, some people think students have a better chance to learn and achieve if they have class only with others of their own sex.

Arguments against separating girls and boys:

* **It's not like the real world.** How many times as an adult do you think you'll work someplace where it's all men or all women?

* **You don't get to hear both sides.** When the two sexes are separated, you only get the point of view of your own sex. This means you don't get to learn what the other sex has to say or see how a boy or a girl might approach things differently.

* **There is less social interaction.** If the two sexes are separated, they don't get a chance to know each other and understand how to get along together.

Some coed schools (schools with students of both sexes) have tried to find a balance by offering classes just for boys or just for girls. These classes are in areas where girls and boys have the biggest differences in learning, like science, math, and English. Teachers can adjust the way they teach to fit the thinking and behavior style that generally works best for people of each sex, without making any one group feel dumb or bored. Yet boys and girls still get to share some classes together, interact socially, and hear each other's point of view.

WHAT DO **YOU** THINK?

If you go to a coed school:

✸ What do you think you would like best about a class with just boys or just girls? What would you like least?

✸ Have you ever wished that there was nobody of the other sex in your classroom? Why did you feel that way?

✸ What would you want your teacher to do differently if you were in a class with just people of your own sex?

If you go to a single-sex school:

✸ What do you think you would like best about a class with both girls and boys? What would you like least?

✸ Have you ever wished that there was somebody of the other sex in your classroom? Why did you feel that way?

✸ What would you want your teacher to do differently if you were in a class with both boys and girls?

No matter what school you go to:

✸ What changes could be made in your classrooms or school that would make it easier for you to learn?

Sometimes, telling a teacher how you feel about school may be helpful. If you have a teacher you're comfortable with, ask her or him if you can talk about the things you've been learning in this book. Don't be afraid to ask questions to discover what your teacher thinks about you, about school, and about gender issues. You might ask:

✱ What do you think is the most important thing for me to get out of school?

✱ What's the hardest part about being a teacher?

✱ What differences do you see between the girls and boys you teach?

✱ How is it different for you teaching boys versus girls?

✱ What would you do if you thought you were treating one sex better than the other?

Make sure to talk to a teacher about specific problems you're having in class. It can help if you keep notes about what issues or topics are troubling you—having notes will help you discuss the situation calmly and keep in mind all the things you want to talk about. It will also help your teacher see that this is really important to you.

What if talking to a teacher doesn't help?

Many teachers want to know what their students are thinking and will be interested to talk about these things with you. But what if that's not true in your case? Maybe you have a teacher who you feel doesn't treat you fairly, and you've tried to talk about it or are afraid to approach him or her. Maybe you're having trouble in a certain class and the teacher isn't giving you the help you need.

If you can't solve your problem by talking to the teacher, don't give up. Talk to another adult who can help you figure out how to deal with the situation—like your dad or mom or a school counselor. If your school doesn't have counselors assigned to students, check at the office to find out who can help you work out a problem with a teacher. (For more information, see "Find out more!" on page 76 and "What can you do about Title IX violations?" page 96.)

Other ways to look at learning

To say that boys learn one way and girls learn another is just too simple. In fact, the way we learn is very complex. One researcher, Howard Gardner, has identified eight ways people think or process information. He calls these "multiple intelligences." All people have ability in at least one of these areas, and often in more than one. These areas of strength are what Gardner refers to as "preferred intelligences." Which one(s) are strongest for you?

 **Linguistic:** People with this intelligence learn best by reading, speaking, telling stories, and discussing things.

 **Musical:** Musical people are sensitive to rhythm, tone, and melody, and like to perform or listen to music, dance, sing, hum, or move to a beat.

 **Logical-mathematical:** This area is strong in people who enjoy solving problems, looking at patterns, and understanding what makes things work.

 **Interpersonal:** This people-oriented approach shows up in boys and girls who get along well with others, like to be leaders, or communicate easily.

 **Visual-spatial:** Someone with this intelligence learns best through pictures, graphs, diagrams, and visual presentations.

 **Intrapersonal:** This is people-oriented, too—but focused on the self. People with intrapersonal intelligence know and understand their own strengths and feelings, set goals, draw or write to express themselves, and often work well on their own.

 **Bodily-kinesthetic:** A person with this preferred intelligence is a natural mover who also likes to handle objects. The person may like gymnastics, sports, dancing, carpentry, crafts, or hands-on science.

 **Naturalist:** Naturalists like plants and animals, are interested in the outdoors, and often like to collect and organize things from nature.

Along with your preferred intelligences, there's still another way to understand how you process information: through your senses. Most people tend to use one of their senses more than the others.

* **Auditory** learners learn best by listening. Their preferred intelligence(s) might include one or more of these: linguistic, logical-mathematical, interpersonal, intrapersonal, or naturalist.

* **Visual** learners learn best by reading or seeing pictures. Their preferred intelligence is visual-spatial, and they may also have strengths in logical-mathematical, intrapersonal, or naturalist areas.

* **Kinesthetic** learners learn best by touching and doing things. Their preferred intelligence is bodily-kinesthetic. They may also have visual-spatial, musical, or naturalist abilities.

Boy *or* girl, it can be really helpful to figure out the ways you're most comfortable thinking and learning. Knowing this can help you in school and in getting along with teachers, parents, and friends. It may also help explain why some things in school don't make much sense to you. And, it can help you see beyond the stereotypes and find out more about the unique way you put your brain and your senses to work for you.

WHAT DO YOU THINK?

* Do you agree that girls and boys learn differently?

* Do you think certain intelligences are generally stronger in boys? In girls? Which ones? Why do you think this?

* How did you decide which of the intelligences are strongest for you?

* Which of your senses do you use when you learn? How is this different depending on the subject you're studying?

* How do you think understanding multiple intelligences and learning styles can help you in school?

Doing school your way

Your sex is your sex. Your strengths are your strengths. Your learning style is your learning style. These things aren't likely to change. At the same time, right now you go to school because you have to. You take certain classes because they're required. Whether you love math or hate it, you need to learn it. Whether English is your favorite or least favorite class, you've got to study it. So why not take advantage of what you know about yourself and use that knowledge to take charge of your learning experience at school? And, while you're at it, why not challenge yourself to move outside of the so-called male or female boxes and try your wings in a few new directions?

One of the great things about being in school is that you're not locked into the rest of your life yet—you probably don't have your study path completely set for the next four or five years, or a career plan already waiting in the wings. You're free to try different subjects and approaches, to work at doing better in some areas, and to take on other things—knowing that even though you may not shine, you can still have fun and learn something new. Now is the time to experiment and stretch. After you graduate, you won't be required to go to school anymore, and suddenly you're going to have to figure out what else you want to do with your life. Your experiences in middle school and high school will give you confidence to do this.

Right now school is your life, or at least a big chunk of it. It's where you spend a large part of your day. It's the reason you get out of bed in the morning. Sometimes, when you're sitting in biology or geography class, it may be hard to see what this could possibly have to do with the rest of your life. In fact, the "rest of your life" might seem so far away that you're not even sure how to think about it. If this is true for you, try thinking about what you're doing right now.

WHAT DO YOU THINK?

* What does being successful at school mean to you?

* How would your definition of success be different if you were the other sex?

In Chapter 2, you looked at traits that people often associate with one gender or the other. Make another copy of the "Gender traits?" form from page 32. This time, look at the traits and think about what it takes to be a successful student. Do two things:

1. Circle the traits that are most important for succeeding in school.

2. Put a star next to each trait you think you have.

When you're finished:

*   Look at the traits that you both circled and starred. These traits are strengths that are helping you in school.

*   Look at the traits that you circled but *didn't* star. These are the traits you might want to work on to help you with school.

*   Look at the traits that you starred but didn't circle. These are traits you have but don't feel are necessarily helpful to you in school. Are there ways some of these traits *could* help you in school? Are any traits causing you problems?

Now take it a step further. Think about the classes you have the chance to take in school. Are there any you'd like to take but avoid because you think they're "boy classes" or "girl classes"? Or because you think you won't be good at them? Yet, doesn't it make sense to work at something you like—even if it seems a little scary? The time and place to start doing that is right now in school. Break some boundaries. Stand up for who you are. Go ahead and take that class where you're the only boy or girl. If you're brave enough to do that this year, then before long there might be other people who follow your example.

School is always better when you allow the real you to come out. Probably the most important thing about surviving school is courage. Don't be afraid to stand up for what you believe, to ask questions, and to grow. The more you can do this, the better you will like yourself—and school.

"No matter what gender you are, you can achieve anything." Boy, 13

Find out more!

Help! My Teacher Hates Me by Meg F. Schneider (New York: Workman Publishing, 1995). The title of this book tells only part of the story. Besides dealing with teachers, the author offers advice on thinking things through, enjoying your school experience, and dealing with grades, homework, sports and extracurricular hassles, sexual harassment, and many other topics.

School Power: Study Skill Strategies for Succeeding in School by Jeanne Shay Schumm, Ph.D. (Minneapolis: Free Spirit Publishing, 2001). This book offers lots of help for boys and girls with reading, writing, and organization. Among other things, it covers how to get your act together, listen and take notes, be a better reader, speak up in class, write right, and study smarter.

DiscoverySchool.com
school.discovery.com/students
This Web site has links to help in all subjects, including BJ Pinchbeck's Homework Helper (a Web site put together by a father and son). You'll find help in all subject areas, including computers (programming, graphics, operating systems, the Internet), science (biology, chemistry, physics), math (general math, geometry, algebra), English (grammar, vocabulary, reading genres), the arts (music, movies, painting), and more. Look for worksheets and study guides as well.

Encarta Homework
Encarta.msn.com/homework
Here's a great site for suggestions on test preparation, writing reports, and improving your writing, with a terrific Web directory for homework help. Also includes help from experts like Ask Dr. Math.

TeensHealth
kidshealth.org/teen
Go to this Web site and click on "School & Jobs" to find "Getting Along with Your Teachers," "Connecting with Your Coach," and more.

Gender-friendly classroom checklist

Mark each statement *usually, sometimes,* or *hardly ever.*

1. Teachers at my school spend an equal amount of time in class talking to boys and girls.
   ❏ usually   ❏ sometimes   ❏ hardly ever

2. Girls and boys get the same amount of time to answer questions before the teacher calls on someone else.
   ❏ usually   ❏ sometimes   ❏ hardly ever

3. Teachers expect the same behavior from both boys and girls.
   ❏ usually   ❏ sometimes   ❏ hardly ever

4. Girls and boys get the same punishments for the same offenses.
   ❏ usually   ❏ sometimes   ❏ hardly ever

5. Boys and girls are encouraged to work together in class.
   ❏ usually   ❏ sometimes   ❏ hardly ever

6. The textbooks at my school have about the same number of pictures of women and men, boys and girls.
   ❏ usually   ❏ sometimes   ❏ hardly ever

7. The textbooks at my school present the viewpoints of both males and females.
   ❏ usually   ❏ sometimes   ❏ hardly ever

8. My teachers and counselors encourage me to explore subjects that may not be typical for my sex.
   ❏ usually   ❏ sometimes   ❏ hardly ever

9. There are about the same number of male and female teachers in my school.
   ❏ usually   ❏ sometimes   ❏ hardly ever

10. There are both women and men in all departments of my school.
    ❏ usually   ❏ sometimes   ❏ hardly ever

Chapter 5

ON THE PLAYING FIELD AND IN THE HALLS: GENDER ISSUES BEYOND THE CLASSROOM

SURVEY COMMENTS:

What did teens write about sports and gender?

"You throw like a girl is an insult." —Girl, 14

"I like to think I am more athletic than girls." —Boy, 14

"People told me that I couldn't play ball because I was a poor, defenseless girl, but I kicked their butts." —Girl, 12

"Girls can play all the sports boys can play." —Boy, 11

"We can play guys' sports, but if guys play girls' sports it's a bigger deal." —Girl, 14

"At school, there are no football teams for girls." —Boy, 12

"When I applied as a newspaper columnist for the sports staff, my teacher wouldn't let me do it because I would have been the only girl." —Girl, 14

"People at school believe girls can't do as well as guys at sports." —Girl, 13

"As a boy, I have more sports opportunities." —Boy, 14

"My gym teacher throws overhand to boys and underhand to girls, even though some girls are better at overhand. And he expects more from boys when it comes to running, pull-ups, etc." —Girl 11

"Some girls act all sissy about sports, and the other girls who like sports are teased or called tomboys." —Girl, 11

"Gym teachers laugh at boys if they can't do something, but are fine with the same thing from girls." —Boy, 14

Girls and boys are equal when it comes to sports, right?

For many teens, sports are a major part of school. Part of the Title IX ruling of 1972 focuses on giving girls and boys equal opportunities in school sports (for more about Title IX, see pages 60–63). It states that both boys and girls are to have similar opportunities to participate in sports—with teams, coaches, equipment, and facilities of equal quality. Why did girls need the support of Title IX when it came to sports?

Before Title IX

BOYS GENERALLY HAD:

- up-to-date sports equipment for each sport
- newer uniforms paid for by the school
- use of the biggest, nicest gym (or first rights to use the only gym)
- transportation to events in a team bus
- practice scheduled after school
- a large athletic budget
- cheerleaders and band performances at games
- higher-paid coaches

GIRLS GENERALLY HAD:

- use of the boys' old equipment
- used uniforms (or they bought their own)
- use of the older, smaller gym (or another space entirely)
- no bus, but needed to find their own transportation to events
- practice early in the morning before school or in the evening after the boys
- a small budget, or had to raise their own money
- no cheerleaders or band support
- lower-paid or volunteer coaches

In 1971, before Title IX was passed, there were about 300,000 girls in the United States who participated in high school athletics, or in other words about 7.5 percent of all the high school athletes. Twenty-five years later the numbers had grown to 2.4 million, accounting for 39 percent of all high school athletes.

That's a big change—especially when you consider there was actually a time when doctors recommended that girls not play sports at all because it might harm their reproductive systems! Opportunities for girls in sports have clearly improved. Still, many of the girls we surveyed wrote about being teased, picked on, laughed at, or called names if they were interested in sports. A few boys also wrote about wanting to take part in physical activities like gymnastics that usually include mostly girls. One boy wrote, "I like tennis and swimming, and some kids think they're girl sports."

WHAT DO YOU THINK?

* Do you think your school offers equal opportunities for boys and girls in sports?

* Which sports at your school attract more attention? Why do you think this is so?

* What has a teacher or coach said to you—positive or negative—that had an impact on the way you see yourself or the way you see sports?

* What's the hardest thing about being in sports for a girl? For a boy?

Your school might be in violation of sports mandates of Title IX if . . .

* your girls' teams are still wearing five-year-old uniforms and playing with hand-me-down equipment from the boys' teams, while the boys get new uniforms and only the best equipment

* the girls have to come to school at 5 A.M. so they can practice and be out in time for the boys to practice

* the cheerleaders go to every boys' basketball game (home and away) but never cheer for the girls' team

* the boys have steak at a sports awards banquet, but when the girls ask for the same thing, they're told the budget won't allow it so they're going to have a pizza party instead

* boys who want to go out for cheerleading or gymnastics, or girls who want to play football or wrestle, are told they can't on account of their sex

Based on our survey, plenty of girls want to play sports of all kinds, but still aren't getting the chance—or take a lot of heat when they do. Though boys didn't have as much to say on this subject, one boy pointed out, "One of my teachers said that a girl couldn't be on the wrestling team because it was against the rules. But I checked and the rules never said anything like that." We read dozens of comments like these from girls:

* "I grew up playing hockey with my uncles and cousins. At school, when I wanted to play with some guys, they wouldn't let me."

* "Some guys say girls are not able to play high-impact or contact sports. They think I can't play football, although I play frequently in my spare time."

* "When I try to play a hard sport like football or hockey, I am often shot down with mean name-calling."

* "All my life I was the only girl on my base-ball team. The pitcher would always throw me the hardest balls. The team all gave me a rough time because I was a girl."

* "People have told me, 'You can't play foot-ball, you'll get hurt.' Sure, but boys get hurt, too."

Certain sports, like hockey and football, definitely seem to be mainly for boys. When girls want to play, they often try to join the boys' team. Coed sports is a controversial subject. It can be uncomfortable for girls and boys to play high-contact sports like football and wrestling together. Both boys and girls can have trouble playing their best if they're worried about touching another athlete in the wrong place. And some people worry that if a team has boys who are bigger and stronger than the girls, girls are more likely to get hurt.

Some girls fight hard for their right to be on the boys' team when there's no similar sport available for girls. Others find ways to play away from school—maybe in community teams or informal neighborhood games. Another idea is to try to rally other girls to form a team of their own. If you are a girl who likes to play football or wrestle, but you're not sure you want to play on the boys' team, why not start talking to your friends. If you're excited enough about your sport you may get them excited about it, too.

Then talk to your gym teacher or another adult at school about starting a girls' team.

GENDER FACT Over 700 high school girls are playing football in the United States, and these girls aren't just kickers, they're also quarterbacks, linebackers, and ends.

So what about the boys? In and out of school, it seems the boys who want to join athletic teams or take part in other physical activities that are typically for girls have it harder than girls who want to play football or hockey. Those strict gender rules society sometimes has are stronger when it comes to boys doing "girl things" than girls doing "boy things." And while many girls feel free to pursue aggressive sports or not, as they wish, boys are under pressure to be good at sports. Both boys and girls in our survey commented on this. For example, one girl wrote, "Dudes are supposed to be jocks and athletes." A boy remarked, "People automatically expect me to be good at basketball. It's hard, because I'm not."

A short history of boys, girls, and cheerleading

1889	The first U.S. cheerleader, a man, leads fans in cheers at the University of Minnesota.
1900–1950	The majority of cheerleaders are boys (it is in the middle of this era that doctors are warning girls and women that strenuous physical activity could be harmful to them).
1950s	Girls start to outnumber boys as cheerleaders.
Today	Nearly 99% of U.S. cheerleaders are girls.

If you look at national and international competitions, you know that some girls and boys *do* break away from the gender roles that can pressure people at school. There are boys who train to be figure skaters and gymnasts, and girls who work to be speed skaters or throw the shot put. Many of these people have had to deal with teasing and criticism in order to pursue their dreams. But they've decided that doing what appeals to them is more important than fitting into society's ideas about what sports are right for males or for females.

Unfortunately, when people of either sex don't take part in athletics, they lose out on some great benefits. Participating in sports helps both girls and boys to

* be healthier

* control anger and anxiety

* learn to take criticism and handle both success and failure

* learn to deal with competitive feelings

* feel more confident

* eat and sleep better

* work as part of a team

* overcome shyness

* set and reach goals

WHAT DO YOU THINK?

* Why is it easier for girls to take part in sports that are traditionally masculine than for boys to join in sports that are considered feminine?

* How would you feel if you were the only person of your sex on a sports team?

* What would be going through your mind if you were on the wrestling team and were asked to wrestle with someone of the opposite sex?

* What would be your arguments for or against coed sports?

How do you play the game?

When it comes to sports, girls and boys might be able to learn something from each other. Since boys and men dominated sports for so many years, sports have long been connected to those masculine traits of leadership, power, and aggression. As girls and women became more involved in sports, some people began to wonder if there could be a place in the game for cooperation, communication, and helping others—traits that are often considered feminine. In her book *Are We Winning Yet?*, Mariah Burton Nelson, a former college and professional basketball player, talks about two ways of looking at sports: the Military Model and the Participation Model.

Sports attitudes and approaches

MILITARY MODEL	PARTICIPATION MODEL
• Being successful means winning.	• Being successful means doing your best.
• Winning is the most important thing.	• Playing is the most important thing.
• Becoming a superstar athlete is what's most important.	• Personal and physical development of team and individual players is what's most important.
• Players are punished and humiliated for making mistakes.	• Players are supported for their efforts and given constructive criticism to help them improve.
• Opposing players are the enemy.	• Opposing players are respected athletes.
• Coaches have absolute authority.	• Coaches and players work together for the best effort.
• Winning is more important than personal health—injuries should be endured and played through.	• Long-term health and physical fitness is important for both the individual and the team.

Of course, these models are about how sports are *generally* played. The ideas don't fit every sport or every situation. They don't mean that all boys who play sports are into making fun of their friends and hurting their bodies, or that boys never care about helping teammates. And they don't mean that girls are never competitive and don't like to shine on the basketball court or the ball field. What the models show are two very simplified views of how people approach sports—two broad ways of thinking that schools, coaches, and players may have in mind when they practice and play. For years, the "winning is everything" or "no pain, no gain" attitude has been the accepted way to play sports. Many coaches have followed this model: you can see it in athletics from Little League to pro games. This point of view is based on those stereotypes that say men have to be powerful, competitive, and ruthless. In this fiercely competitive climate, boys and men are called "girls" or "sissies" if they don't do well. Remarks like these hurt a boy's self-confidence. They can make him feel angry on and off the playing field, and can make sports seem a lot less fun.

Sometimes in sports people have to make tough decisions. Consider these situations:

Just suppose . . .

Your basketball team has made it to the semifinals. In the previous game, you fell and hurt your knee. The doctor told you that it's only a slight sprain, but that you should stay off of it for three days. The next day, your coach says you need to play anyway because you're the top scorer for your team. Your knee still hurts. What do you do?

• • •

You are the assistant coach for a girls' softball team. Your younger sister is one of the players. She's been working on her batting, but she still has a lot of trouble hitting. It's the last inning of the game and you are down by one run. You have a runner on third and two outs, and it's your sister's turn at bat. The head coach is thinking of putting in a pinch hitter and asks for your opinion. You know your sister will be really hurt if you take her out of the lineup. What do you do?

Maybe it's hard for you to figure out what to do in each case. Maybe it's easy. Your choices can tell you something about your own personal approach to athletics. Some people don't like a more cooperative attitude toward sports. They worry that if winning isn't the most important thing, games will stop being competitive altogether. In the Participation Model, though, winning is still important—it's just not the *only* important thing. Some coaches feel that this newer approach actually makes their teams more competitive: It seems to help the athletes be more healthy, relaxed, and self-confident, and the result is that they often do better than teams where people play with injuries or where coaches and teammates use put-downs as a way to motivate.

The point here isn't to argue that everyone should start playing every game following the Participation Model or the Military Model. There could be parts of each style that girls, boys, their coaches, and their fans might benefit from. As with masculine and feminine gender roles, you don't need to choose one or the other. The idea is to see that the traditional way of doing it isn't necessarily the only way. Recognizing this can give you more choices, depending on the particular situation.

WHAT DO YOU THINK?

* If you play or watch sports, what do you like best about them? What's the most important part of sports for you?

* At your school, do the teams seem to follow more of a Military Model or a Participation Model? Is this different for boys' teams and girls' teams? For each sport? In what ways?

* How does your attitude change depending on the game you're playing? On what's happening in the game?

* When you play other types of games, like video or board games or cards, what model do you follow? Why?

* Do you think attitudes about competition spill over into other areas, like friends or school? In what ways?

Choir, yearbook, drama club: Where are the boys?

You've seen that more girls continue to take part in sports, although boys still participate more than the girls. What about other activities? In many cases, when it comes to non-sports extracurricular activities, the opposite seems to be true—boys are underrepresented.

Who participates?

The National Federation of State High School Associations gathered information about school activities from two-thirds of U.S. states. Here's some of what they learned about who's participating in what.

ACTIVITY	GIRLS	BOYS
drill team	80%	20%
vocal music	68%	32%
orchestra	63%	37%
dramatics	61%	39%
band	56%	44%
debate	52%	48%

Why do more girls take part in things like choir and theater while more boys take part in sports? One reason might be the brain and hormone differences that mean boys are generally more physical and aggressive while girls are typically more verbal and emotional. (See Chapter 2, pages 22–28, and Chapter 4, pages 63–67.) Another reason might be those limit-

ing gender roles and stereotypes that put pressure on people to do "girl things" or "boy things." As a boy wrote in his survey, "In school, you'll get made fun of if you're a boy who does girls' stuff."

Think about the activities in your school. Are some more popular with girls? With boys? Are there any activities that people of both sexes seem to enjoy?

And what about elements within the activities? For example, who plays which instruments in the band or the orchestra? Are there some instruments in your school band that most people consider to be mainly for boys or for girls? How do students react when a boy decides to play a flute or a girl decides to play the trombone?

What kinds of plays draw more girls or boys for try-outs? Are there language clubs in your school? Do more boys or girls tend to take certain languages or join certain language clubs? Who plays chess? Who's on the staff of the yearbook? The literary magazine? Who reports on which subjects for the school paper?

What activities interest *you?* The whole point of outside activities is to follow your interests, try new things, and get to know new people. It makes sense to do those things that appeal to you, and it makes sense that girls will like some activities a little more while boys will prefer some others. On the other hand, sometimes the fact that something seems to be more for one sex or the other can keep you from trying an activity you'd like to do. Now, we don't mean to suggest that you should sign up for something that doesn't even appeal to you, just to be "gender-correct." But don't be afraid to take a risk. If something interests you, go for it!

Here's something to try with a friend or two. On the left side of a sheet of paper, list the activities you take part in both at and away from school. On the right side, list activities you don't take part in now, but think you'd like to try. For each item, think about why you like (or why you might like) the activity and what you can learn from it. Talk together about this. Do you and your friends think the activity is mainly for boys, girls, or teens of either sex?

WHAT DO YOU THINK?

✱ Think of an activity that seems to attract more girls than boys. Why do you think girls prefer this activity?

✱ Think of an activity that seems to attract more boys than girls. Why do you think boys prefer this activity?

✱ What are some of the best activities to do with people of your own sex? With people of both sexes? Why?

✱ Is there an activity that interests you but that you're nervous about trying? What's keeping you from trying it? What might happen—good or bad—if you tried it?

Sexual harassment and Title IX

Another issue covered under Title IX is sexual harassment. In 1997, the U.S. Department of Education conducted a study called "Title IX: 25 Years of Progress." The study found that even after years of having a law that says students aren't supposed to be taunted or bullied at school because of their sex, sexual harassment of students by other students is still a big concern. In fact, it's a problem that's growing, not shrinking.

Many times people get harassed or bullied because they don't fit into the narrow gender roles that people have set up for boys and girls. At school, students may make fun of other students because they don't look, dress, or act "like a girl" or "like a boy," or because their bodies are fully or not-so-fully developed. This kind of harassment is called sexual harassment. Sometimes a boy or group of boys will harass a girl or a group of girls. Sometimes it's the other way around. Sometimes, too, it's girls harassing other girls or boys harassing other boys.

No matter who's doing it, it's sexual harassment when someone makes remarks that are meant to be negative about gender roles, bodies, sexual activity, or sexual orientation. *Sexual orientation* refers to whether people are straight (heterosexual), gay or lesbian (homosexual), or bisexual (sexually attracted to people of both sexes). For more information on sexual orientation, see pages 147–149.

Sexual harassment takes many forms, including

* name-calling, dirty jokes, comments about breasts or erections, and other verbal harassment

* touching or grabbing

* staring

* spreading sexual rumors

* cornering someone

* writing sexual graffiti about someone

* following or stalking someone

* sending sexually explicit letters, notes, or emails

* yanking on underwear or snapping bras

* making obscene sounds or gestures

Sometimes sexual harassment can become such a normal part of your life that you don't even realize it's there. In his book *Real Boys' Voices,* William S. Pollack said that when he asked boys if they had ever been sexually harassed they said no; then, when he asked them if they had ever been called "wuss," "wimp," or "fag," they told him that happened all the time, that it was just part of being a boy. Guess what? That's sexual harassment. And while it may seem like it's just part of being a boy, that's not the way it should be. Sexual harassment hurts.

You may also have noticed that a lot of sexual harassment involves using slang words for homosexuals. *Homophobia,* the irrational fear of homosexuals or of being gay or lesbian, is very prominent in our society, especially among men, and also among teenagers, both male and female. Harassment based on homophobia can happen to anyone—straight, gay, or bisexual. Some people will make fun of anybody who acts outside of those narrow gender roles society sets by labeling them lesbian or gay, whether this is the case or not.

Some of the students wrote about this in the survey. One boy admitted, "There was this girl, and I called her a lesbian because she dressed like a boy." Another student wrote, "Because I'm a boy and I act the way I do, people actually ask me if I am gay."

Why does homophobia exist? Often people make fun of others in this way because they are anxious or troubled about their own sexuality. They know they don't have *only* masculine or *only* feminine traits themselves, but maybe they think they should, and so they worry about whether they're "all-boy" or "all-girl."

GENDER FACTS

* In a national U.S. survey, 4 out of 5 students (both girls and boys) reported experiencing some type of sexual harassment at school.
* More than 1 in 4 students say they are often sexually harassed.
* A study of students in public high schools found that 97% of teens reported regularly hearing anti-gay comments from their classmates.

Teenagers who are openly gay are often the targets of harassment. To avoid getting picked on in this way, gay and lesbian teens often hide their feelings. This means they can end up thinking no one understands or cares about who they are. They often feel very alone and confused, and can get depressed or even suicidal. These are serious consequences caused by some people's cruelty and unwillingness to accept different ways of being a girl or a boy.

Title IX has rules that protect all students from sexual harassment, including harassment based on sexual orientation. Title IX protects you from being harassed by other students, and also by teachers or other adults at school. According to Title IX, it is illegal—against the law—for someone to sexually harass a person so that

1. the person's school performance is affected **OR**

2. the person feels like the environment at school is sexually intimidating, hostile, or offensive

Anyone who's ever been sexually harassed at school, or has seen someone else who has been harassed, knows that it can have a big impact on how you do in school. It's hard to concentrate on a test or class discussion if you're thinking about the hurtful things that someone has said to you in the hall. It can be tough just making yourself get out of bed and go to school if you know people will harass you when you get there.

Flirting v. harassment: What's the difference?

Sometimes people who have been accused of sexual harassment say that they were only joking or flirting. So what's the difference between sexual harassment and flirting? It can help to keep this in mind:

> **Sexual harassment is about the way the person who receives the sexual attention feels about it. It is *unwanted* attention.**

Flirting: Flirting is a give-and-take kind of thing between two people who are attracted to each other or who enjoy each other's company. When someone flirts with you, it can make you feel good about yourself, attractive, and self-confident. It can leave you with one of those smiles on your face that causes people to ask you what you're thinking about.

Sexual harassment: When you're being sexually harassed, it's no fun—there's no give-and-take, it's all one-sided. Instead of feeling attractive and self-confident, you feel self-conscious and put down. People who've been sexually harassed don't go around smiling about it. If you think you're being harassed, then you are.

Sometimes what seems like flirting to you might feel like sexual harassment to someone else. Does this mean that you're never supposed to flirt with anybody? No—it wouldn't be much fun if people could never flirt! If you're not sure whether you've crossed the line from flirting to harassment, ask yourself these questions:

* Did the other person respond favorably to what you said and did? Or did the person ignore you or seem upset or embarrassed?

* How would you feel if someone said or did the same thing to some body in your family?

* Why were you flirting? Were you more interested in how the other person felt or in scoring points with your friends?

* How would what you said or did sound if a reporter were telling a story about it on the evening news?

* How would you feel if the roles were switched? Would you like the way you'd been treated?

Dealing with sexual harassment at school

If you're being harassed:

Do something to stop the harassment. Most people who have been sexually harassed say that they just ignored the harassment. Ignoring something doesn't make it go away.

* Tell the harasser how you feel and ask the person to stop. If you are afraid to do this, ask a friend or trusted adult to talk to the person with you.

* Write a letter to the harasser stating exactly what the person has been doing and asking that it stop.

* Find out if your school has a sexual harassment policy. If it does, report the harassment to school administrators or teachers, following the school's reporting guidelines. If there isn't a clear policy, find out who your school's Title IX coordinator is. In the United States, each school district is required by law to have a person who serves in this role. Your school principal or dean can tell you how to contact the coordinator or how to file a report about what has happened. In your complaint, be sure to give detailed information about the harassment, including where and when it took place and any action you took to stop it. Ask witnesses to make reports, too, or to go along with you for support.

If you see someone else being harassed:

* Support the person being harassed. Tell the person that the harassment is illegal and that there are things that can be done to stop it.

* Make a public scene. Confront the harasser and say that the behavior is *not* okay. Get other people to go along with you. A lot of times people keep on harassing because nobody has called them on it.

* If you're a girl and another girl is doing the harassing, or if you're a boy and another boy is doing the harassing, you may also want to apologize to the person being harassed on behalf of the other members of your sex.

* Report the harassment to the school administration, and ask others who have witnessed it to make reports, too.

If you've been harassing someone:

* Stop.

* Apologize to the person you've hurt.

* If you don't know why you've behaved as you did, or if you're having trouble stopping the harassment, talk to someone who can help you, like a parent, trusted teacher, or counselor.

A school where harassment regularly takes place without any consequences is a school that doesn't really care about its students. People have been known to skip or drop classes—even quit school—when sexual harassment has gotten out of control. If harassment is a problem at your school, do something about it. Take a stand by forming a school organization to help solve the problem and make the halls and classrooms of your school a place that feels safe for everyone.

WHAT DO YOU THINK?

* What do you do when you hear or see harassment taking place?

* Have you ever been sexually harassed? How did it feel? What did you do?

* Have you ever sexually harassed someone? If so, did you do it on purpose? What do you think was going on that made you choose to harass someone? How could you handle things differently next time?

* What do you think you could do to make your school a safer and less hurtful place for all girls and boys?

What can you do about Title IX violations?

Title IX applies to what goes on all over your school, from the classrooms to the cafeteria and from the halls to the gym and playing fields. It requires schools to treat students of both sexes equally in and out of class, in the bathrooms, in locker rooms, on school grounds, and during sports and extracurricular activities. If you notice something that seems unfair in your school, take action.

* If the problem is with a teacher, a coach, an activity advisor, or another adult, talk to the person or write the person a letter. If you write to the person, keep your own copy of the letter. Be sure that you explain what's bothering you and give specific examples. Many times people don't even realize that they've been treating someone unfairly, and when it's pointed out to them they'll try to change what they're doing.

* If going to the person directly doesn't help, or if you're not comfort able doing so, talk to another adult that you trust, such as a counselor, another teacher, your principal, or your mom or dad.

* If the problem is with a school policy—or the lack of one—get the support of a teacher or school administrator to help you take steps to make a change.

* If people don't listen to what you have to say or refuse to change their behavior, you can file a formal complaint with the Title IX coordinator. (This person is available for all complaints, not solely issues of harassment.)

* Keep looking and asking until you find a person who will help you.

"Everyone should be treated equal. It really doesn't matter what gender you are, what race you are, or what you're good at. EVERYONE is equal." Girl, 12

Find out more!

A Sporting Chance: Sports and Gender by Andy Steiner (Minneapolis: Lerner Publishing Group, 1995). This book shows the history of girls and women in sports from Little League to the pros, tells individual athletes' stories, and gives clear information about Title IX. It will give you a complete picture of the hurdles girls have crossed and continue to face when it comes to equal participation in sports.

GirlHealth
www.girlhealth.org/content/ri_harrass.html
GirlHealth is a site created by young women for young women. This section on sexual harassment describes what sexual harassment is, what to do when it happens, and where to go for help.

Chapter 6

HIP OR HYPE? WHAT'S THE MESSAGE IN THE MEDIA?

SURVEY COMMENTS:

Do teens think media and popular culture (TV, movies, magazines, music, and clothes advertising) affect their ideas about what it means to be a boy or a girl?

 "You get the idea that boys are tough figures, always after a girl. The girls seem always to be snippy and stuck-up. I'm not all those things all boys 'should' be, and I know girls aren't either." —Boy, 14

"I think the media affects some people's opinion, but not mine." —Boy, 12

"What we wear, what we do—all the cool trends come from the media." —Girl, 12

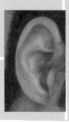 "Commercials point out and exaggerate the differences between genders. Kids learn to think that way." —Girl, 10

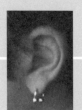 "I personally don't think that all people match the way girls and guys are portrayed." —Girl, 14

"The media kind of makes me think that guys have to be athletic and girls have to fit in with everyone." —Girl, 11

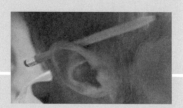

"Yes. Kids act differently depending on what's popular on TV." —Boy, 14

"These things all affect us, whether people think they do or not." —Boy, 16

"Popular culture makes both sides have no respect for the other." —Girl, 13

"People are surrounded by popular culture, and it's like osmosis—it sinks in." —Girl, 14

Magazines, movies, music, and more

You may not even have to leave home to feel the effects of some of society's strongest gender stereotypes. All you have to do is turn on the TV or radio, log on to the Internet, pop a CD into the player, open the newspaper, or flip through a magazine. Away from home, just look out the bus window at the signs and billboards on the way to school, or check out the logos and labels on the clothes and gear of everyone around you.

These things are all part of the *media*. The media is pretty much everywhere, keeping you informed, entertained, and connected. Can you imagine a day when you wouldn't come into contact with media and all the messages it contains about popular culture (what's supposedly in or out, hot or not)?

The media reflects society's ideas about lots of things—particularly about what it means to be male or female. And it doesn't simply *show* these ideas: it works hard to *shape* them, to get people to feel that there are particular ways men and boys, women and girls, are or should be. Think about all those . . .

. . . **video games** where men and boys (and the occasional tough babe) get to blow up stuff.

. . . **comic books** with buff, sexy, all-powerful superheroes who usually use violence to save the day.

. . . **magazine quizzes** with titles like "What's Your Shopping Style?" or "Are You Winning the Dating Game?"

. . . **music videos** where sultry, sexy people come on to each other, or big, mean males talk crudely about the women in their lives.

. . . **ads** that pop up on the computer screen inviting you to try the very latest guy- or girl-catching product.

. . . **TV shows** where girls gossip and plot viciously against each other while groups of boys belch, tell jokes about sex, and break things.

You may wonder: But a better question might be:

> "Who **are** these people?"   "Whose **ideas** are these?"

There's definitely a message about what's supposed to be important to boys and to girls. Sometimes the message seems to be that you're not the girl or boy you *should* be, that you're not feminine or masculine enough.

♂ Boys' view: For boys, violence is something that occurs over and over again on television, in the movies, in video games, and in comics. Aggressive competition is part of the thrill of sports, but television coverage often emphasizes injury and conflict over skill. Wrestling shows can feature more taunting and humiliation than actual physical prowess. Boys also tend to enjoy physical and "gross" comedy, and much of the humor on TV and in movies is about sexual stereotypes. And what comes on between segments of TV shows? Beer ads with men drooling over sexy women, or car commercials that show men who are either hip or outdoorsy driving vehicles that are either suave or rugged. What does all this suggest about boys?

♀ Girls' view: When it comes to girls and women in the media, the message seems to be mixed. On the one hand, TV and movies often portray smart, honest, independent girls and women who solve their own problems and care more about the world around them than about their looks. On the other hand, many of these competent women and girls fall apart when a cute male catches their attention. Much of what's on TV and in movies, music videos, and magazines tends to reinforce those stereotypes that say women and girls are silly, sexy, and man-obsessed. Often, too, these media show girls and women as victims of sexual and physical violence.

One example of the mixed message about girls is in video games. Lots of video games portray tough women who face challenging missions. But take a look at these women! They have exaggerated breasts and tiny waists, and they fight their battles in skimpy, tight clothes.

There are other ways the media keeps feminine stereotypes alive and well. One is simply by showing fewer females than males. (You'll notice this in nearly all media except magazines geared specifically to girls or women.) They also do it by showing more women than men who are interested in dating and getting along with the other sex and more men than women in roles that are about their job or their work. And they do it by sending messages about what the ideal female looks like and about how important appearance is in girls' and women's lives. All over the media, there are far more females than males who do things like worry about weight, cry, whine, flirt, and act weak or helpless. And there are far more older males than older females.

Media numbers

How many people of each sex are actually shown in different kinds of media?

CATEGORY	MEN	WOMEN
video games	84%	16%
music videos	78%	22%
movies	63%	37%
TV commercials	58%	42%
TV programs	55%	45%

Who's dating or talking about relationships?

CATEGORY	MEN	WOMEN
TV	17%	23%
movies	16%	27%
commercials	4%	9%

Who's going to work?

CATEGORY	MEN	WOMEN
TV	41%	28%
movies	60%	35%
commercials	17%	9%

Maybe it seems like we're giving the media too much credit. After all, TV, movies, and even ads are meant to be entertaining. Are they really that harmful? Does the media intend to shape popular culture and influence people's thinking? Many of the students who responded to our survey thought so.

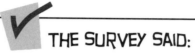

THE SURVEY SAID:

53% of boys said popular culture affects people's ideas about what it means to be a boy or a girl.
67% of girls said popular culture affects people's ideas about what it means to be a girl or a boy.

WHAT DO YOU THINK?

* Do you feel that the media affects some people's ideas about what it means to be a girl or a boy? In what ways?

* Does it affect *your* ideas? Why or why not?

* What are some of the things the media seems to be telling girls they should be like? What boys should be like?

* How are you like the image the media has of your sex? How are you different from this image?

What's on TV?

TV can be great. It's always there to amuse you, tell you exciting stories, and keep you in the know about what's going on in the rest of the world. So what is that little glowing box saying about gender roles? Think about some of the dramas and sitcoms you watch.

How do girls and women act? Are there more strong, capable female characters than dumb or ditzy ones? How are the women dressed? How often do women and girls on TV

* take care of themselves?   * talk or think about sex?

* talk or think about relationships?   * talk about clothes?

* make jokes about men or boys?   * dis their friends?

* look sexy, try to, or wish they did?

How do men and boys act? Do you see many men who are tough guys? Strong, silent types? How are gay men portrayed? When male characters show their feelings, how do they do it? How often do men and boys on TV

* fight and/or use weapons?   * talk or think about sex?

* talk or think about relationships?   * talk about sports?

* make jokes about   * look macho, try to, or wish
  homosexuality?   they did?

Another interesting thing to notice on TV is the commercials. Shows that are geared to teenage girls and young women usually have commercials for lingerie, hair color and shampoo, chick-flicks, diet sodas, and foods that help you stay thin. Ads that are shown during the programs intended for teenage boys are often for sports shoes and gear, sports drinks, action movies, cars and trucks, and pizza. Shows for teens of both sexes advertise music, zit-zapping lotions, and clothes.

Of course, there are lots of different kinds of shows on TV, and *all* of them don't stereotype girls and boys. Still, when you put the shows and commercials together, those messages about what it means to be a girl or a boy come through pretty clear.

And when you watch TV, what characters remind you of any real people you know? Many times the lives of kids from a wide range of ethnic backgrounds, kids who don't have much money, or just ordinary everyday kids don't get shown very much. Or, if they do, they are portrayed as exaggeratedly uneducated, crude, boring, or bumbling.

Here are some of the comments people wrote on our survey about the images they see of men and women on TV.

TV males, TV females

GIRLS SAID:	BOYS SAID:
"Girls are portrayed as giggly little freaks obsessed with hair and makeup."	"Boys are portrayed as rebels and girls as conformists."
"It's sad how much we strive to be thin like the girls on TV."	"Boys look and act like tough guys or fools."
"A five-year-old can watch TV and think that is how she should dress or look to be attractive or noticed."	"We're supposed to think that if a boy has a good body like in music videos, he may be more popular."
"Most boys' basketball and baseball are shown on TV—not girls'."	"On TV, guys are always heroes and girls are always helpless."
"In the music videos, boys always seem to get these really pretty girls who are all over them."	"Guys are the ones that do the cool stuff, and the girls are the bimbos wearing bikinis."

The thing about TV is that, for the most part, it's fake. You know it's fake. The people who produce the TV shows know it's fake. Actors are hired not only for their acting ability, but for their appearance—to embody an image the producers want to show of particular ways to be male or female. Programs are written to be dramatic or funny, not necessarily to show things the way they really are. Still, it's easy to get caught up in the lives of the characters and imagine yourself in that perfect, exciting, funny, or hip TV world. Some people even strive to look and act like the people they see on TV. When this happens, real life can start to seem boring, and the real you can seem to not quite measure up.

Here's an activity you can use to see what shows pass the reality test. You can do it on your own, but it might be fun to try this with your dad or mom, sister or brother, friend, boyfriend, or girlfriend. Choose some of your favorite TV shows, or some of the most popular ones. Make several copies of the "Gender roles on TV" form on page 120 to fill out whenever you watch TV for the next week or two. As you watch, pay close attention to the characters. Notice how they look, what kinds of jobs they have, how they relate to each other, and what sorts of gender roles they play. Do they seem like real people—people you know? Give each program a reality ranking based on a scale of 1 to 10, with 10 being most realistic.

After each show, compare notes. If you like, take it a step further by copying and filling out the form on page 121, "My TV awards."

WHAT DO YOU THINK?

* What, if anything, surprises or bothers you about gender stereotypes you see on TV?

* Which male or female characters on TV show positive gender roles? What is it about them that you admire?

* Can a comedy be funny without using gender stereotypes and jokes about males and females? Why or why not?

* Can an action drama be exciting if it's not violent? Why or why not?

* Is there a place for gender stereotypes on TV? Do they serve any kind of positive purpose? What?

Wouldn't it be nice to be so important and powerful that you could name which programs earn the awards? The truth is, when it comes to TV, you may have more power than you think. Advertisers, the people who keep interrupting your shows with commercials, want you to buy their stuff. They're paying lots of money to put their ads on during the shows you watch. If people aren't watching a show, they're not watching the commercials; if that happens, the advertisers aren't willing to pay to run ads on that program. This means that if enough people quit watching a certain show, it won't stay on the air. It's that simple.

It doesn't hurt to keep this in mind when you're watching the tube. Do you have some favorite shows you hate to miss, and then other shows you watch when you're just bored? Pay attention to what's actually on the screen when the TV is on. If it's something you'd rather not support—turn it off!

There's another way you can let studio execs know what you think about their shows. Maybe you have a favorite show, but you wish the writers would change some of the ways the characters act. Maybe the show you love used to be good but has lost its charm for you. Maybe you really like a show and feel it isn't getting the support it deserves. All the major networks have a Web site along with email and snail-mail addresses where you can write with your feedback and ideas. (You'll find several of these listed on page 119.) You can tell the network producers if there are things you'd like to see more of on TV and what issues you'd like to see dealt with. If there's a show you don't like, you can let them know why.

Most of us enjoy TV. But watch smart. Choose the programs you really enjoy—the ones that help you feel good about yourself, that show people in ways you like to see people portrayed, or that let you laugh at life's twists and turns without making fun of people.

Now playing: Take a closer look at the movies

Every weekend thousands of teens grab some friends and go see what's playing at the local multiplex or head out to the video store to rent a stack of movies. As a group, teenagers go to movies more than anyone else. Because of this, many movies made today are aimed at teenagers. Often PG-13 movies are actually intended for preteens, and R-rated movies (which aren't supposed to admit anyone under seventeen) are targeted for young teens. Teen movies typically fall into one of several categories.

Comedy

Likeable, often goofy, people (usually guys) get themselves or others into embarrassing-yet-funny situations. People in positions of authority try to get them in trouble. Funny/goofy person wins in the end (often ends up with the most beautiful girl). Or smart kids get the best of stupid adults.

Date movie (aka romantic comedy)

Two very attractive people who are obviously meant for each other meet, immediately dislike each other for some reason, and spend the rest of the movie figuring out that they belong together, at which point they live happily ever after.

Action movie

Good guy(s) v. bad guy(s). Usually the bad guy has hurt (or plans to hurt) someone who the good guy cares about. So the good guy has to protect that person (usually a woman) and then get revenge. To do this, the good guy often has to hurt/kill many other people—but that's okay, because he's the good guy. Once in a while the good guy or the bad guy is a tough, sexy female.

Scary movie

Attractive teenagers try to have sex and get chased and killed by a psychotic killer. A girl in a skimpy outfit is usually the prime target, but if she's been having sex with her boyfriend, he's probably going to get killed, too. Surprisingly, a girl is often the only one left at the end of the murder spree, which is usually, but not always, committed by a guy.

Teen sex comedy

Basically one or more very attractive virgins (girls) or pathetically out-of-it virgins (boys) try their best to *lose* their virginity, while at the same time drinking lots of beer and doing stupid and/or disgusting things.

Preteen feel-good movie

Spunky girl wants to get away from her confining world. She meets a guy who's ready to rescue her, but there's usually some sort of catch (example: he's a beast with a nasty temper). Or smart-but-drab girl helps popular guy but remains an outsider until he discovers the "real" her—usually with a new haircut, makeup look, and knockout outfit.

STEREOTYPE ALERT! Does it seem like we're doing some stereotyping here? It's hard to talk about stereotypes without making generalizations, and those generalizations can start to sound like stereotypes! So keep in mind that this is a broad way of looking at typical kinds of movies. These things are often true, but not always. In general, boys and men get to be the heroes, and sometimes they just look stupid or foolish. Occasionally, a woman gets to be the hero—someone smart and strong who is able to take control of the situation. More often, though, girls and women have minor parts to play, are sex objects, or are portrayed as caring mostly about whether the boys and men like them. Sometimes you'll see movies that are more realistic, but not very often.

Movies are made to entertain. They distort real life for dramatic effect (and try to tell a story in under two hours). Of course, in real life

* Boys/men don't have to blow up something or shoot someone to show that they care

* Girls/women think about more than boys/men and clothes

* Violence and negative risks and behavior hurt people

* Sex has consequences

* Mean jokes and pranks hurt

* After people fall in love, the story doesn't end

* Not all women are five foot seven and weigh 110 pounds

* Not all men are six feet tall with sculpted shoulders and six-pack abs

Almost without knowing it, as with TV, you might find yourself looking at movie characters and celebrities as ideal people with traits and lives you wish could be yours. But who can live up to a Hollywood view of life that takes hundreds of people and millions of dollars to create? As for happy endings, think about a great experience you've had. If your life had been a movie, the film would have stopped right there at your peak moment. Then you wouldn't have had the chance to go on and do all the other cool things (or hard things—they're tough, but they're real) you've done since then.

And just like television, it's $$$ that drive the movie industry. When it's your money you're paying to watch a movie, make sure it's something you really want to see. Next time you rent movies, try watching like a critic. Photocopy and use the TV gender role and award forms on pages 120 and 121 to figure out which movies are real and which show positive gender roles.

WHAT DO YOU THINK?

* Why do people watch movies? What makes them enjoyable?

* Who is your favorite male or female character in a movie? What do you like about this character?

* Look at the ads for movies in the newspaper. Can you tell by looking at the ads if the movies will use gender stereotypes? What do the ads tell you the female and male roles will be like?

* How can movies be funny, dramatic, or scary without gender stereotypes?

Magazines: Decoding the hidden messages

Magazines can be hard to resist. They scream at you in bright colors and funky fonts. They promise the answers to finding love, fitting in, and looking great, topped off with celebrity gossip. But what do they really have to offer?

♀ Girls' view: The magazines for teenage girls are pretty easy to spot. All of them are usually grouped together on the shelves. They often have pastel covers with pictures of smiling, fresh-faced female models, or this year's hottest young actor. They feature articles about embarrassing moments, the latest makeup and clothing styles, and how to attract or keep a cute guy.

♂ Boys' view: Magazines for teenage boys are a little harder to spot. Unlike for girls, there don't seem to be any general-interest magazines geared to teenage boys. This means that a lot of boys end up buying magazines that are written for men. Some of the men's magazines most popular with teen boys are all about being macho, with a mix of photos of scantily clad women and articles about sex, money, and violence. There are also dozens of specialty magazines about cars, sports, computers, and gaming. Along with sex, these magazines include articles about extreme behaviors and lifestyles. The publishers of these magazines know that a large portion of their audience is teen boys.

There are also some magazines that could appeal to both girls and boys, especially music, entertainment, and some sports magazines. But for the most part, magazines are written for an audience that falls at either end of the gender continuum. There are many things that boys and girls have in common, but try telling that to a magazine editor or an advertiser!

WHAT DO YOU THINK?

✱ Why do you think there are so many magazines geared to teen girls and so few geared to boys?

✱ If you were to publish your own magazine, what would it be called? What kind of articles, pictures, and ads would you put in it?

Now, think about advertising for a moment. Have you ever opened a magazine to look for that article that sounded so interesting on the cover, only to flip through page after page after page of ads before you could even find the table of contents? All those glossy magazine pages have to get paid for somehow, and the publisher does that by selling ads.

Take one of your favorite magazines and try this experiment:

1. Write down the headlines on the cover.

2. Count the number of pages in the magazine.

3. Count the number of pages with ads in the magazine. Subtract this number from the total number of pages to see how much content the magazine actually has. (Another way to look at this: to see what you've actually paid your three, four, or five dollars for!)

4. Make a general list of the things the ads are selling (example: clothes, food).

5. Compare what the ads are selling to the types of articles. Is there a connection?

What exactly are the publisher and advertisers trying to sell you? Mostly they're trying to sell you short on yourself. In order to want to buy something, you have to feel like you need it. You need to feel like there's something in your life that will be missing if you can't have that particular product. You have to feel like you're not good enough, not pretty or handsome enough, not cool enough. Here are some of the kinds of products that have ads in magazines for girls and boys and what these ads say to you.

Advertising messages

BOYS

Product	Message
video games	Playing video games teaches you how to be tough.
deodorant	Real guys need strong deodorant.
clothes	If you don't have clothes like these, girls will think you're *so* out of it.
shoes	If you're going to play, you have to have the right shoes.
trucks/cars	Real guys drive trucks, SUVs, or sports cars.
audio/video stuff	Boys have to have their toys.
sports	What red-blooded North American guy isn't into sports?
cigarettes	Smoking is manly and sophisticated.
alcohol	Women love guys who drink. Beer is especially macho.

GIRLS

Product	Message
perfume	How do you expect to get a guy smelling like *that?*
makeup	You're not nearly attractive enough without help.
clothes	If you don't have clothes like these, guys will think you're *so* out of it.
facial hair bleach	Ooh! What's that *thing* above your lip?
hair color	Guys won't notice you with that drab hair.
mouthwash	No offense, but your breath could offend that special someone.
blemish reducer	Zits! Gross!
monthly medication	You're no fun to be around when you're all moody and bloated.
lip gloss	Nobody would want to kiss lips like yours.

Many magazines targeted for boys are actually for men, so they can get away with advertising you won't find in girls' magazines, for example, ads for cigarettes and alcohol.

Advertisers want you to buy their product. The magazines need the advertisers to buy ad space in the magazine. If you're happy with who you are and how you look, you're less likely to want to buy the products because you won't feel like you need them. So the magazines are full of articles telling you (in a highly positive way) that you're simply not good enough. For girls, not being good enough = not being attractive enough. For boys, not being good enough = not having what it takes to be a man. Advice columns, exercise and weight lifting programs, makeovers, interviews with sleek starlets and tough guys—they're all designed to make you feel that you're not quite the person you ought to be. Then, right next to these articles on how to make yourself a much hipper girl or boy, what do you find? What else? Advertisements for products that can help you be prettier, tougher, sexier, and closer to perfect.

To get even more perspective on the ads in magazines, put yourself in the place of an alien from another planet. Photocopy and fill out the "Magazine humans" form on page 122.

Now, WAIT a minute . . .

. . . lots of people think it's pretty fun to change the way they look, fool around with hair color and styles, try out different exercise programs, and see what's new in clothes. They like reading about movie and sports celebrities, finding tips in advice columns, and taking quizzes to see what they know about the other sex or how they measure up in the romance department. They enjoy finding out what other teens and preteens have to say in the letters to the editor and Q&As. As a matter of fact, people go to college and pursue careers in sports, fashion, and advertising. Maybe you're even thinking of doing this one day. Are we really suggesting everything about it is all bad?

No. But just like their glossy covers, many magazines are all about surfaces. They don't get into the complexities of who you are. And in many cases, it's in both the advertisers' and the magazines' best interest for you not to like who you are. The truth is, many advertisers *do* prey on people's feelings that they're not good enough. And many magazine ads and articles perpetuate gender stereotypes that don't fit all girls or all boys.

As a smart person, you can tell whether advertising is responsible. You can recognize gender images you like and don't like. The point is to start paying attention and to decide for yourself what's right for you and what's not.

Here are some of the things people who filled out the survey said about ads and other media messages.

THE SURVEY ASKED:

Think about a teen-related ad, magazine cover, music video, or movie you've seen. How did it portray boys or girls?

BOYS SAID:

"Most ads portray the guy like owning the girl. I don't like this."

"The ads are pretty much all the same. The girls are super-good looking and the guys have all this muscle."

"On all the magazines, there are pictures of very nice-looking boys. Not all boys are athletic and good looking."

"There's always something about a guy saving a girl and being a hero."

"Movies portray boys as ill-mannered people who go around killing people all the time."

"They all show boys as drooling animals who only think about girls and sex."

GIRLS SAID:

"Teen ads show girls as skinny and not wearing enough clothes and guys as being 'in control.'"

"Magazines show girls in skimpy clothing looking lifeless, like just a body. Guys are usually doing something athletic—which makes them look like a living thing."

"In most movies it's the guy who saves the girl or the world. The girl does all the crying. It's dumb and sexist."

"Movies show girls who care about school as geeks, girls who are into art as goths, and the girls who don't care for school as popular. It makes it seem like you have to lack interest in school to be accepted. That is not true."

"They always show half-naked girls in music videos, and movies show nude scenes of girls, never guys."

"Boys and girls are both portrayed as sex symbols."

How do you feel about your body?

Have you ever been having a really sweet day, feeling good about yourself and how you look? And then you sit down to watch TV or look at a magazine, and suddenly you just don't feel so sure of yourself anymore? That's because TV, movies, magazines, video games, and ads tend to show an image of perfection that is literally impossible to live up to.

Even the actors and models, who are hired because they are supposedly so beautiful or handsome, aren't really attractive enough on their own.

"Hello, I'm a model."

See all my trendy clothes? Someone else picked them out for me.

I have a professional trainer who exercises with me every day and helps me choose the right kinds of foods to eat, so I won't get any ugh! body fat.

A professional hairstylist cuts and styles my hair.

A professional makeup artist carefully applies makeup to cover up any flaws so I can look even more perfect.

Somebody dresses me, to make sure all my clothes fit just right.

During my photo shoot, the hairstylist and makeup artist stand around and wait in case my hair or makeup gets messed up, so they can "repair" it.

After the photo session, the computer people look at the pictures and "fix" any little lines on my face, erase any sign of body fat, add color to my eyes, make my pupils larger, tweak my hair so it's smoother or messier, and do lots of other tricks to make sure I have just the right look.

I guess it's a good thing I'm naturally attractive.

Of course, nobody could be expected to live up to the image of these idealized female and male bodies. But many people, both boys and girls, try to every day. Sometimes it can be hard to like your body when you're faced with so many images of "perfect" people.

♀ Girls' view: Studies have found that as many as 40 percent of nine-year-old girls diet or have habits associated with eating disorders. These girls already have the idea that their bodies aren't right! The focus on getting thin leads girls to try fad diets like eating only meat or only fruit, or to take diet pills, which can be dangerous for anyone who isn't being supervised by a doctor. There are also lots of girls who do what's called yo-yo dieting—take off weight, then gain it, then take it off again. This kind of dieting isn't good for a person's body, either, and can lead to weight problems when you're older.

Sometimes dieting can lead to serious eating disorders like anorexia or bulimia. With anorexia, a person starves (or eats very, very little) to stay thin, and sometimes overexercises to burn calories. Anorexia includes having a distorted body image: the person sees fat in the mirror, even though there isn't any. With bulimia, a person binges (eats way too much) and then purges (throws up or takes laxatives). Eating disorders like these can cause serious health problems, and even death—all from trying to achieve a goal that's impossible to reach.

♂ Boys' view: Many people think that dieting, poor body image, and eating disorders are only a problem for girls, but boys deal with these issues, too. While images of the perfect body for girls are all about being thin, for boys they're about being muscular, tough, and macho. Think of all the times you've seen photographs of men and boys with their shirts off, showing off their chiseled chests and bulging biceps. Boys are more likely than girls to abuse steroids in order to build up their muscles and do better in sports, and the number of teenage boys using steroids is growing. Steroids involve many health risks: they can reduce sperm, shrink testicles, halt bone growth, and damage the heart, liver, and kidneys.

WHAT DO YOU THINK?

✱ How do you feel about your body? In what ways do you think you're affected by the body images you see in the media?

✱ Think about one part of your body that you like. It can be anything— your eyes, your hair, your toenails. What do you like about that part?

✱ Think about your least favorite body part. Why don't you like it? Is it really a problem, or is it something that's unique to you and perfectly okay? If it's a problem, how could you make a change? If it's not a problem, think of a way to change how you view it. One idea is to make it silly. If you can laugh about it, maybe you can even start to like it.

✱ How do the things you watch, do, and read help you feel good about being a girl or a boy? How *don't* they help?

If you don't like your body

Eating disorders and poor body image don't happen just because people try to look like celebrities and models. Disliking your body can be related to other problems, like depression, low self-esteem, or family troubles. If you feel seriously worried or bothered about anything related to your body, talk to an adult and get some help. At the end of the chapter (page 119), you'll find resources specifically for eating disorders. You can also call the 24-hour National Youth Crisis Hotline toll-free at **1-800-448-4663.**

10 tips for becoming media-savvy

So how can you start to get past these images of who you "should" be to connect with the great person you really are? You've already started doing the most important thing—paying attention. When you really begin to notice what's being said and shown to you, instead of just quietly listening or looking, you can start to interpret what's going on. The following guide will help you tune in to what the media is trying to say to you and what you can do about it.

1. **Turn on your reality meter.** When you watch TV or movies or read articles in magazines or on the Web, ask yourself: Do the people, characters, or models talk, act, or look like people I know? What's realistic or unrealistic about them?

2. **Be on the lookout for gender roles and stereotypes.** Are boys and girls generally shown in traditional male and female gender roles? Or are they allowed to be like real people and behave in many different ways?

3. **Know the good stuff when you see it.** Some good stuff to look for:

   ✱ real people who make both good and bad choices and have to face the consequences of those choices

   ✱ both girls and boys having the opportunity to "save the day"

   ✱ stories or lyrics that put boys and girls in roles that go beyond stereotypes

   ✱ positive role models

   ✱ things that push you to think for yourself and to believe in yourself

4. **Look at the advertising.** Is someone trying to sell you something? How is the ad, article, song, or show trying to convince you that you need a certain product? Does the advertising play on gender roles? How does the advertising affect what you're looking at or listening to? Are girls and boys depicted as real people or "perfect" ones?

5. **Notice your feelings.** As you watch, read, or listen, how do you feel about yourself? Good? Bad? Angry? Depressed? Excited? Confused? Bored? Why do you think you feel this way? Does realizing how you feel make you think differently about watching, listening to, or reading this particular thing again?

6. **Talk about it.** When you have strong feelings about something in the media, talk about them—with your parents, your teachers, your classmates, your friends, your boyfriend, or your girlfriend. By sharing your views, you might help someone else see something in a new way. Plus, you'll get to hear what other people think.

7. **Look for alternatives.** If, after paying closer attention, you find that you're not very happy with something you once enjoyed, look for alternatives. There are good magazines, movies, TV shows, CDs, music

videos, and Web sites out there. Things that are written for teens, by teens, can be especially good.

8. **Make your own alternatives.** If you're feeling especially creative, start your own magazine. Build your own Web site. Write your own songs. Join your school's newspaper or news team if there is one. See if there's public cable access, or local newspaper features or TV programs for and by young people. This way you get to choose what you want to say and how you want to say it.

9. **Speak up.** If you don't like what's going on in the media, tell someone who can do something about it. Write, call, or email people in charge. You can easily look up the address or Web site of your local TV and radio stations. CDs and magazines often have the address of the producer or publisher right on the cover or near the table of contents. Many movies have Web sites that list the name of the producing studio. Video games should have producer contacts on their packaging or at their Web sites. If you really want to make an impact, tell others how you feel and encourage them to speak up, too.

10. **Take action.** Anything that keeps you from being a passive observer of all the things that are coming at you is taking action. If a TV show, magazine, or band is feeding you destructive images, don't watch, read, or listen to what it's selling. You can stop buying products that use advertisements telling you you're not good enough. If you get really ambitious, you can even start an official boycott and get other people to stop buying products with offensive advertising or watching shows or listening to music that present stereotypes or limiting messages.

   If you find good magazines, TV shows, or movies that express who you really are and present positive images of girls and boys, tell people about them. Don't keep the good news to yourself.

"Just because a magazine says that this song is popular and therefore you should like it, or these clothes are popular and therefore you should wear them, it doesn't mean I'm going to do that. I have my own views and my own opinion." Boy, 13

Find out more!

National Association of Anorexia Nervosa and Associated Disorders (ANAD)
www.anad.org
ANAD's free services include a newsletter, educational programs, and information on support groups and referral sources. You can call Monday through Friday (9 A.M. to 5 P.M. CST) at (847) 831-3438.

National Eating Disorders Association
www.nationaleatingdisorders.org
This organization developed when the American Anorexia Bulimia Association (AABA) partnered with Eating Disorders Awareness and Prevention (EDAP). Check out their Web site to find general information about eating disorders and body image concerns, tips for helping a friend avoid or deal with an eating problem, and treatment referrals to treatment centers, doctors, therapists, support groups, and more. Or call them toll-free at 1-800-931-2237.

TM Voice
www.tmvoice.com
This is the Web site for TM (Target Market), an organization that was started by a group of teens in Minnesota. TM produces advertising and actively campaigns against cigarette advertisers. Check the site for news, membership information, facts about tobacco advertising and legislation, and ways to get active or "Kick Ash."

Here are addresses and Web sites for major TV stations:

ABC, Inc.
500 S. Buena Vista Street
Burbank, CA 91521-4551
abc.com

CBS Television Network
51 West 52nd Street
New York, NY 10019
cbs.com

ESPN Television
ESPN Plaza
Bristol, CT 06010
espn.com

MTV Studios
1515 Broadway
New York, NY 10036
mtv.com

NBC Entertainment
Viewer Relations
30 Rockefeller Plaza
New York, NY 10112
nbc.com

20th Century Fox Theatricals
P.O. Box 900
Beverly Hills, CA 90213-0900
fox.com

Gender roles on TV

Program name:_____

Characters:

Name_____ Sex _____ Age _____

Race/Ethnicity_____Job/Main activity_____

Name_____ Sex _____ Age _____

Race/Ethnicity_____Job/Main activity_____

Name_____ Sex _____ Age _____

Race/Ethnicity_____Job/Main activity_____

Name_____ Sex _____ Age _____

Race/Ethnicity_____Job/Main activity_____

Program's gender reality rating: _____

Why it gets this rating:_____

_____

_____

_____

_____

_____

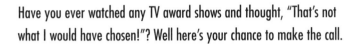

My TV awards

Have you ever watched any TV award shows and thought, "That's not what I would have chosen!"? Well here's your chance to make the call.

Most realistic TV show for teens (drama): _____

Most realistic TV show for teens (comedy): _____

Strongest female character (adult): _____

Most sensitive male character (adult): _____

Strongest female character (girl/teen): _____

Most sensitive male character (boy/teen): _____

Least realistic TV show for teens (drama): _____

Least realistic TV show for teens (comedy): _____

Character most like me: _____

Character least like me: _____

Character I would most like to have for a friend: _____

Character I would least like to have for a friend: _____

Best female role model: _____

Best male role model: _____

Most interesting gender-role reversal (examples: a man who cares for children or a woman who's an

adventurous scientist): _____

Magazine humans

Imagine you're from another planet and have been asked to go observe people on Planet Earth. Before making the trip, you decide to research what human females and males are like by looking at magazines. What do the magazines tell you?

Magazine male:_____

_____

_____

_____

Magazine female:_____

_____

_____

_____

When you get to Planet Earth, you go to a school somewhere in North America. How do the real humans in the school compare to the magazine humans?

Real teen boy:_____

_____

_____

_____

Real teen girl:_____

_____

_____

_____

Chapter 7

MAKING CONNECTIONS: GIRLS, BOYS, AND THE SOCIAL SCENE

SURVEY COMMENTS:

What unwritten social "rules" do teens think apply only to girls or to boys?

"Boys are supposed to be ladies' men or sports stars to be cool. Girls have to be thin and cute and flirtatious to be popular." —Boy, 14

"Girls: Be nice and sweet. Boys: Be strong, tough, and cuss." —Girl, 13

"Boys can't cry, they have to punch back if they get punched, and they can't talk about their feelings too much." —Boy, 16

"For a girl, if you put down others, you're cool. You're either with the preps or the uncool kids." —Girl, 14

"Unwritten rules for boys: NEVER cry or show defeat, NEVER admit to your mistakes, and never give affection or comfort to others." —Girl, 12

"Rules for girls: Don't act too friendly with boys, and try to fit in or get snubbed." —Girl, 16

"Sometimes a really pretty girl gets called a slut, but it's not like that for guys. If a guy is good looking, he gets respect." —Boy, 14

"The unwritten rules for girls are: Don't act boyish, wear girly clothes, laugh at all the guys' jokes, and make guys feel better about themselves." —Girl, 16

"Girls are expected to be what the guys want, but it doesn't always happen that way." —Boy, 13

Are the social "rules" different for boys and girls?

With the Internet, email, phones, cell phones, and pagers, it seems like people are constantly trying to stay connected with each other. All of those gadgets we use to stay in touch are pretty cool, but the really important thing is people and how they communicate and get along.

Just like everything else in your life, the messages you receive about being a girl or a boy play a part in how you connect with other people. In Chapter 3 (pages 47–50) you read about unwritten rules that exist in families—strong ideas or expectations about how girls or boys ought to be, act, or think. The social scene at school is another place where gender expectations play a big role. We explored this in the survey by asking about what we called unwritten social "rules." We wanted to know if teens felt their friends and classmates had ideas about how boys or girls should act in social situations.

THE SURVEY SAID:

43% of girls said there are unwritten rules that apply to girls.
32% of girls said there are unwritten rules that apply to boys.
30% of boys said there are unwritten rules that apply to boys.
25% of boys said there are unwritten rules that apply to girls.

A majority of both girls and boys felt there *weren't* unwritten rules, yet many still told us their ideas about how people in school expect girls or boys to behave socially.

Girl friendships, boy friendships: What's the difference?

You've probably noticed that girls who are friends act differently with each other than boys who are friends. Behavior experts have studied how boys and girls get along with other people of the same sex and they've noticed differences, too. One difference starts in childhood: When young children of both sexes play together, they often tend to do things that are "gender neutral," like play board games, put puzzles together, or finger paint. But when girls play with girls, they tend toward more typically feminine play, while when boys play with boys, the activities tend to be more typically masculine.

So what happens as kids get older? Are teen boys' friendships all that different from teen girls' friendships? As with most things, the answer is an indisputable "maybe." Here's a list of behaviors that experts have found to be often (but not always) true when it comes to boys who are friends and girls who are friends.

Friendship

What's different?

BOYS WHO ARE FRIENDS TEND TO:

- do something first, and talk about it later

- push, shove, roughhouse, and otherwise physically goof around with each other
- build or fix something, or play a game or sport when they hang out together
- recognize one boy as the leader within the group
- yell and fight physically when they disagree

- not show or talk about their feelings and problems with each other

GIRLS WHO ARE FRIENDS TEND TO:

- make plans and arrangements first, then get started

- discuss the issues that are important in their lives
- do activities that express who they are (photo albums, journals) or how they look
- form partnerships and work together

- fight with words (gossiping, name-calling), snub each other, or break alliances
- show and talk about their feelings and problems with each other

What's the same?

Whatever their differences, most teens agree that both boys and girls want friends who:

- are loyal
- can be trusted
- accept each other for who they are

- are honest with each other
- care about, understand, and support each other

Of course, not all girls and boys fit these descriptions. Still, when it comes to friendships among boys or among girls, it's hard to argue that some differences don't exist. If you look at some of those differences, you'll notice that there are both positive and negative things in each case.

♂ **Boys' view:** One boy wrote on his survey, "Boys have to one-up each other all the time." Because many boys grow up playing or following sports, boys learn that competition is important. They also learn about relying on a leader, being part of a team, and getting things done. Remember how little boys are encouraged to be loud and rowdy? Most carry this message into their teen years. Lots of boys goof around, play physical pranks, like rude humor and in-your-face music, and roughhousing. On the survey, boys said how much they enjoyed these aspects of being male, and wrote: "It's great to spit and swear," "I like to get outside and be rough," and "Boys rock!"

When it comes to emotions, though, boys sometimes find it easier to talk with a girl than with their closest male friend. Why? Because they feel she'll be less likely to make fun of them and may be better able to understand their feelings. Some boys simply would rather *not* talk about their feelings at all, and are glad not to be pressured to do so. As one teen boy wrote to us, "The best thing about being a boy is that I can be left alone when I'm in a bad mood."

When boys get mad at each other, you usually know it. Rather than talk first, they often go right to insulting each other, arguing, yelling, pushing, shoving, or even slugging. In one way, a direct or physical approach is honest—both sides know they're angry, and the fight is usually over fairly quickly. But put-downs and hitting don't fix everything; bad feelings can fester, and violence can escalate.

Slugging and shoving don't help boys learn how to discuss and work through problems that really need to be solved. The physical approach gets boys in the habit of using size, strength, and power to make their point. As a boy, you might be able to get away with a punch between friends, but that method won't help you work out a problem with a parent, teacher, boss, coworker, or girlfriend. Plus, a larger or more athletic teen can intimidate those around him. A teen with a less-imposing build might even go along with something he'd rather not do to avoid a physical confrontation.

While most adults teach otherwise, fighting is still seen by some as an acceptable masculine way to react to a problem. There are plenty of messages from the media to remind us that "might is right." Teen boys who opt not to fight, either by choice or because they are at a physical disadvantage, risk having their masculinity questioned. (You'll find information about dealing with anger on pages 23–25.)

♀ Girls' view:

Like boys, girls can have a lot of fun together, even if the things they're doing are sometimes different. Lots of girls wrote in the survey about the importance of friendship. One said, "The best thing is having so many friends who are girls. We have so much fun." Another wrote, "I think girls typically have deeper friendships."

It seems like girls can talk with their friends about *anything*— which boys sometimes envy. One girl explained, "When boys think about something, like if they have a problem, they don't tell their friends, but girls do." Another agreed, saying, "It just doesn't seem like guys are as close as girls are." But sharing so much emotion can have both an upside and a downside. Girls can be "friends forever" one moment and not talking the next.

Even though girls may find it easy to talk about feelings and problems, they don't always deal well with being angry at each other. Many girls are taught that it's unacceptable to get into physical fights. The same social "rules" that tell boys fighting is okay tell girls to "play nice" and *not* fight. So while boys are more likely to take the physical approach when dealing with disagreements, girls have learned more subtle strategies. "Girls gossip more," noted a girl on her survey, "and they judge more than guys." Girls will ignore each other, spread rumors, or say bad things behind each other's back. These actions can hurt just as much as a punch or hard shove—and can take longer to heal. As one girl wrote, "I don't want my friends to talk about me." Another put it even more broadly: "I would change girls to make them less cruel to others."

Being able to cooperate and share feelings can improve friendships for boys and girls alike. So can learning to be assertive and honest. And hurting people—with words, fists, or silence—is bullying. Bullying isn't a foundation for friendship or for being your true self.

BULLY FACTS   * In one national study, 38.7% of boys reported that they'd been in a physical fight within the last twelve months. Overall, male students were significantly more likely than female students to fight physically. The number of girls fighting physically appears to be rising, though.

* Researchers are learning that girls aren't necessarily less aggressive than boys—they just show the aggression in different ways. Up to the age of four, girls tend to fight like boys do, by grabbing, hitting, or pushing. By the time they're eleven or twelve, they're more likely to do things like write nasty notes, spread rumors, and say mean things.

WHAT DO YOU THINK?

* In your experience, is there a difference between girl friendships and boy friendships? If so, what do you think is the best and worst thing about boys' friendships with boys? Girls' friendships with girls?

* Think about a group of friends that are of the other sex. What do you like about their friendship?

* If you could change one thing about how you and your friends get along, what would it be?

* When you have a problem with a friend, how do you deal with it?

The group thing

Being friends in a group may not be as personal as spending time with a best friend, but it can have its advantages. When you're with a bunch of friends, you get to spend time with a variety of different people. You might feel more confident, too. Going to the mall with a group of kids, boys and girls, might seem easier than asking one person out on a date. You might even like it when people associate you with the people you hang out with.

Many people think that only the popular teens hang out in groups, but there are all kinds of groups. Groups often form because the people in them have something in common. Maybe they all went to the same elementary school, play on the same sports teams, like to surf or snowboard, enjoy computer games, are into the same kind of music or clothing styles, or feel strongly about a particular issue like racism or drunk driving. Some groups are mostly girls, some are mostly boys, and some are made up of both boys and girls. For example . . .

A group of girls who are all athletes might become friends and start to hang out together. Their time together may be spent talking about sports, training, exercise, coaches, and all those things that have to do with athletics. Within the group, the girls may have very different inter-  ests, too. Maybe one girl is a singer, another loves science, and another likes to read mysteries. Still, when they're together, they think of themselves mainly as athletes, and tend not to let their other sides come out.

A group of boys might love skateboarding. They can spend hours perfecting moves, playing video games, following the X-games, searching skateboard sites on the Internet, creating Web pages with cool graphics and sound effects, and developing their own style. The boys in the group might like the same bands and wear similar clothes. They probably have other interests as well. One boy may like to run, another might play the guitar, and another could be a writer. Within this group, though, all the boys focus on what they have in common: skateboard culture.

A group of girls and boys get together to play extreme Frisbee, go to the movies, meet for pizza, or just hang out at a coffee shop. Everybody knows each other and the atmosphere stays pretty casual. The boys know they can look to the girls for advice or someone to talk to, just as the girls know they can count on the boys. Sometimes, two people in the group become a couple, but nothing ever gets too heavy or uncomfortable. Mostly they all just  have fun, hang out, help each other study, and support each other's activities—like watching a boy perform in the school play, or cheering for the girls on the track team.

Maybe you mainly hang out with boys, with girls, or with both. Doing things in mixed groups of girls and boys is a good way to get to feel comfortable with the other sex. And if you've ever wondered why boys or girls always seem to do this or that, who better to ask than your male or female friend?

Sometimes groups emphasize the differences in gender roles. If you're a girl and hang out with a group that's mostly girls, you might find yourself being pressured to act more "girly" than you normally would. If everybody is talking about clothes and boys, that's what you'll want to talk about in order to be accepted.

It's the same for boys. Several boys on our survey talked about being pressured to do "manly" things. When they were with a group of boys, they felt like they constantly had to prove themselves. "A guy can't act like a girl or talk about girly things," remarked one boy. "If someone was doing that, I would think something's wrong with him." Another boy wrote, "Some things are stupid, revolving around peer pressure. For example, if someone is new at your school, you have to beat them up."

The old saying that there's power in numbers is true. With a group behind you, when life gets rough or you need a little courage, you can feel more confident and in control. Your group can have power over *you* as well, though. They can influence the way you dress, the things you buy, and the way you act. Groups can help you have an identity, but they can take it away, too.

If you've ever had a group of kids at school turn against you, then you know how powerful the group can be. A group of people that sets itself apart from others, makes it difficult for other people to join, and gives group members a hard time for being a little different or for hanging out with anyone who's not part of the group is a clique. Cliques are cruel, not cool. Sometimes individuals who would never pick on somebody on their own find themselves ganging up with their group to bully, intimidate, or intentionally embarrass others. These bullying behaviors can use fists or weapons, words or rumors, even vicious pranks.

You could probably make a whole list right now of all the different types of groups in your school. You very likely belong to one yourself, even though you may never have thought of it that way. You might even belong to some cliques.

Groups v. cliques

What's the difference?

IN A GROUP:	IN A CLIQUE:
• people like to hang out together	• people give members a hard time for spending time with kids outside the group
• everyone's friends are welcome and people can do their own thing	• only those with the "right" look, interests, or status are included
• you know where you stand	• you could be declared in or out at any time
• people have fun doing stuff with each other	• people make fun of others and feel superior
• you spend time with people in the group because you like them	• you're in the group because you're afraid of what they'll say about you if you're not

People who took the survey wrote quite a bit about cliques. One teen told us, "As a boy, I always think that I have to do what everyone else does and try and fit into the crowd." Another person wrote, "One of the unwritten rules at school is that some girls can't talk to the more popular girls. There are basically two groups of girls at school, popular and scrubby."

WHAT DO YOU THINK?

✱ What kinds of groups are in your school? What kind of cliques?

✱ What group(s) do you belong to? What do people in your group(s) have in common? Can anyone join? What do you do together?

✱ Is there a group you want to be a part of but aren't? What do you think you'd like about being in this group? What wouldn't you like?

✱ Do you think your group expects girls or boys to act a certain way when they are with the group? If so, how are they expected to act?

✱ How does the way that others in your group see you influence the way you act as a boy or a girl?

✱ What are some ways you act differently with teens of your own sex than with teens of the other sex?

You may find it hard to go against the group you're in, or to step in when you witness a group's cruel actions toward others, because you risk getting the same hurtful treatment. You might even convince yourself that targeting someone to be treated badly is harmless fun ("Everybody does it") or necessary (someone "asked for it" by dressing a certain way or by making a particular remark). But you'd be wrong. Not everybody is unkind and disrespectful toward others. And no one deserves to be hurt, humiliated, lied about, or treated like a nonperson.

Sometimes in a group, members don't feel comfortable questioning poor treatment of others or risky activities because they fear being hurt or ridiculed. This isn't a group where friends care and support each other. It may seem that the price you'd pay for speaking out against what's going on (drawing attention to yourself, angering your friends, setting yourself up for similar treatment) is too high. But the price your school as a community pays is even higher. Isolation can lead teens to depression, substance abuse, and even attempted suicide. Attempts to "get back" can lead to school shootings.

CLIQUE FACTS

* According to a U.S. nationwide poll of fourteen- to seventeen-year-olds, 77% of teen respondents reported that there are students who are "above the rules" in their schools. 36% say that the students with the most influence engage in frequent or constant intimidation or embarrassment of students who are not part of their groups/cliques. 41% say there are no consequences for this type of behavior.

* More than two-thirds of the teens polled reported that there are groups of students at their school who intimidate others with few or no consequences. While many victims of harassment and bullying respond by isolating themselves, almost a third of respondents said victims usually plan ways to get back at their intimidators.

Take an "individuality check"

Did you ever hear the saying "Go along to get along?" Have you ever done something with your group that you probably wouldn't have wanted to do on your own? Like try something dangerous, stupid, or embarrassing, or make someone else feel bad? Next time your group wants to do something you're not so sure about, take an "individuality check." Ask yourself these four questions:

* Am I being pressured?

* What would my mom/dad/favorite teacher think about this?

* What effect will this have on others or on my future?

* What other choices do I have?

If you're not happy with the answers to those questions, don't go along with the group. If you're in a group that's pressuring you a lot of the time, it might be good just to get away every once in a while. Find time to spend with a friend who will let you be yourself, or alone doing something you like to do that maybe your friends don't share.

Cliques and bullies only have the power others give them. Don't make it so easy for them. You can help make your school a safe place to learn and have fun with friends. Here are some things you can do to begin:

* Get together with other girls and boys who want to help make school safer and friendlier for everyone.

* Ask a teacher or another adult to work with you.

* Find out if your school has a peer mediation program or problem-solving group. If it doesn't, start one. The student council or community leadership programs, such as the YMCA, YWCA, or Boys and Girls Clubs of America can help, too. (For more information about these groups, see pages 150–151.)

* See what other teens are doing to take the hate out of school. Check out the "Responding to Hate at School" Web site developed by the Southern Poverty Law Center *(www.tolerance.org/rthas/index.jsp)* and the site for the Colorado School Mediation Project *(www.csmp.org/peermed/peer_home.htm)*. Or find out about SHiNE, a program that's part of the White House Campaign Against Youth Violence (see page 171).

* Arrange a school assembly on peer intimidation, cliques, and conflict resolution.

* Put up posters or organize a mural project encouraging everyone to honor difference, include others, and treat each other with respect. Consider displaying a "Wall of Support" in the school's common area featuring the signatures of students committed to saying no to intimidation and bullying behaviors.

* Publicize your efforts over the PA system, in the school newspaper, and in local hangouts like coffee shops and pizza places.

If you're being bullied, intimidated, or harassed

When it comes to any kind of bullying or harassment, the suggestions on pages 94–95 can help. Remember: You are not alone, you can get help, and you can make it stop.

WHAT DO YOU THINK?

Take some time to talk to your friends about how they see your group. Here are some questions you might talk about.

* How do you think other people see our group?

* Does gender play a part in how we act and think as a group? In what ways?

* Do you think we ever ignore or exclude people, on purpose or not? If so, why?

* How supportive are we of each other? Do we stand up for each other enough? In positive ways?

* What's the best thing about our group?

* What could we do to make our group even better?

* Is it easy or hard for people in our school to cross lines and hang out with different groups? Why?

Real friends

Real friends can be male or female. They accept you for who you are and make you feel better, not worse, about yourself. They won't intimidate you or pressure you into doing things that make you uncomfortable. This is true whether it's a close friend who wants you to smoke, a group of friends who expect you to be mean to someone, or a person you're going out with who wants to go further sexually than you do.

Some teens feel like the girl in our survey who said, "Girls and boys can't be just 'friends.'" But they can, if the reasons for their friendship are honest and mutual and if they trust and respect one another's feelings. Actually, this is true for any good friendship.

In Chapter 2, you looked at traits that people often associate with one gender or the other. Make another copy of the "Gender traits?" form from page 32. This time, look at the traits and think about what it means to be a real friend:

1. Circle the traits that you think are most important for being a good friend.

2. Put a star next to each trait you think you have.

3. Think about your friends, and ask yourself which of these traits they have. Put a check mark next to those "real friend" traits you think the people you hang out with have. Do this for friends of both sexes.

Real friends, male, female, or both, care about each other. If you're in a relationship where things don't feel right, where the give-and-take isn't there, ask yourself if it's a healthy friendship. This list of warning signs can help you decide.

A relationship is unhealthy if a friend . . .

* doesn't like you to spend time with anyone else

* makes fun of you in front of other people

- accuses you of seeing other people behind his or her back
- tells you what you should or shouldn't wear
- drives your other friends away by insulting them
- criticizes your beliefs
- makes you feel that nothing you do is ever good enough
- spies on you when you're apart
- tells you you're stupid
- makes unreasonable demands
- threatens to hurt herself or himself if you break off the relationship

If something like this is happening to you, you need to get out of the relationship. Talk to an adult you trust, someone who can help you and maybe get help for the other person involved.

WHAT DO YOU THINK?

- Do you have the traits you'd like to have in order to be a good friend? What can you do to build more of these traits?
- Do you look for the same traits in male friends and female friends? Different traits? Why?
- Which friends have which "real friend" traits? What do you appreciate about these friends?

Boys, girls, and boundaries

One thing that you may find different with girls versus boys is boundaries. A boundary is a limit, an invisible line that separates things. In sports, crossing the line, or boundary, is a clear technical call. You're either over the line or you're not. For people, boundaries are personal and not always clear. Some people, such as a teacher or parent, might have specific boundaries and expectations. There's no confusion: you know when you've stepped over the line by not handing in homework or missing curfew. Other times it's not so clear. For instance, suppose you're teasing a friend about something he or she is wearing. At first the friend laughs with you. But then you say one thing too many, and the person gets mad or embarrassed. At that point you've crossed a boundary, and what you're saying isn't funny anymore.

People's boundaries change depending on who they're with. And—surprise!—gender roles relate to boundaries, too. Most people have boundaries in three areas: touching, privacy, and embarrassment. These are areas where it is especially important to be aware of other's boundaries when you're with boys or girls.

Touching. The way girls touch each other and the way boys touch each other can be pretty different. For instance, girls often like to give hugs. It isn't at all unusual for them to hug a friend when they're excited, sad, or just saying hello or good-bye. A boy, on the other hand, might get very mixed sig-

nals if a girl hugs him in one of these situations. He might be relaxed about it, he might be uncomfortable, or he might think the girl is hinting at becoming more than friends.

Boys rarely hug other boys. The boys on the basketball court, however, might give each other a slap on the hand, a punch on the chest, or a smack on the butt after a good play. Teammates understand this as a friendly touch that basically says, "Good job." But if boys and girls were playing hoops together, a boy's slap on a girl's butt might not be welcomed or clearly understood.

The boundaries of touching are unwritten rules, and the rules can vary. They depend on the person and the moment. You may think you're touching someone in a completely harmless way, only to find out that you've crossed a boundary with the person. A person may not even think twice before grabbing your hand or smoothing your hair, but you may not like this at all—even if it would be okay coming from someone else.

Privacy. Privacy covers a lot of territory, from who you let go through your backpack or gym bag to who knows what about whom. There are certain things you might consider nobody's business but your own. There are some things you might share with only your closest friends or with your boyfriend or girlfriend. And there are other things you might share with only girls or only boys. Privacy is a big issue for most teens and, as with touching, its limits vary a lot from person to person and from situation to situation.

Embarrassment. What embarrasses one person and what embarrasses another may be different. Still, everyone deals with embarrassment. Body functions—from burping and farting to periods and erections—give both boys and girls plenty of embarrassing moments. Having people find out something you didn't want them to know can be embarrassing, too. So can being called on in class when you don't know the answer or you're not prepared. If you misunderstand someone, if someone misunderstands you, if  you say the wrong thing at the wrong moment, if someone criticizes you in front of other people—all of these situations can be miserably embarrassing for everyone involved.

The most helpful way to react when someone gets embarrassed is to think about how you would feel if you were in that person's place. Sometimes the kindest thing to do is just pretend you didn't notice. At other times, you might want to reassure the person that you don't think it's a big deal. There are even times when a joke can help ease the embarrassment. The same suggestions can help if you're the one who's embarrassed. You might say, "Oops, now *that* was embarrassing!" or "Excuse me." You might simply say nothing. Or, you might have a laugh.

So what are *your* boundaries? Maybe you're not sure. Take some time to think about where you draw the line in terms of touching, privacy, and embarrassment. Talk about it with your friends. It is interesting to see how the various people in your life define their own personal limits.

WHAT DO YOU THINK?

✱ How would you finish each of these sentences?
  It's okay with me when someone . . . and NOT okay when someone . . .
  Private things I share with certain friends include . . .
  Private things I keep to myself include . . .
  I feel embarrassed when . . .

✱ Which of your boundaries are different with boys or with girls? Why?

✱ Think of a time when someone made you uncomfortable or you made someone else uncomfortable. How did you handle the situation? What else could you have done?

✱ How can you tell what other people's boundaries are?

Once you're clear about your own boundaries, how do you let others know what they are? What can you say if you or someone else has stepped over a line—or if you're not sure where the line is? Here are some words you might use to get started:

✱ "I want you to know that I'm not mad at you, but it makes me uncomfortable when you . . ."

✱ "I may not have ever told you this, but I don't like it when people . . ."

✱ "Because you're such a good friend, I want you to know that . . ."

✱ "I think I embarrassed you at lunch today. I didn't mean to make you uncomfortable, and I'm sorry."

✱ "I noticed the other day that it seemed to bother you when I hugged you. Am I right?"

✱ "Do you mind if I look for a pen in your purse?"

✱ "Does it bother you if I talk to you about this?"

✱ "Would you rather talk about this later, in private?"

✱ "I know you didn't mean any harm, but it was really uncomfortable for me when you teased me in front of Maya."

If a friend embarrasses you, touches you in a way that makes you uncomfortable, or invades your privacy, speak up. It might hurt the person's feelings at first, but it could save a lot of problems later. And if it's turned around and a friend asks you to respect a boundary, don't be offended. If you sense that you've made someone feel awkward, apologize. When people can be honest about these things, everyone will feel safer and more comfortable.

There will probably be times when you'll cross a boundary without meaning to. And just because you know where a boundary is today doesn't mean it won't be different tomorrow. Boundaries can change over time or depending on a person's mood. That's why it's so important to always be clear about where your personal boundaries are, and to figure out what's okay and not okay with other people—girls *and* boys.

More than friends: Double standards and mixed signals

You've had friendships your whole life, but the older you get the more likely it is that you're forming relationships where you're more than friends. Starting to think about somebody else in "that way" can be wonderful—and confusing. Knowing what to say or what to do can be challenging. Your friends may have expectations for you that you don't share, like dating a certain boy or refusing to date a particular girl. Your dad or mom may start asking if someone who calls is your "girlfriend" or "boyfriend." Or they might think that dating of any kind can only mean dangerous behavior on the road to ruin.

Keep this in mind: The same things that are important to any friendship—honesty, caring, mutual admiration, and respect—are important in a more-than-friends relationship. Being attracted to someone because she's popular, or because he always wears the coolest clothes, or because your friends have decided that this is "the one" for you, isn't part of the recipe for a successful relationship of any kind.

When it comes to dating and romance, there are a few myths and misconceptions we could all do without.

Myth #1: Girls and boys can't be friends.

Reality check: Not only is this not true, but the most successful couples are usually friends. Part of the boys-and-girls-can't-be-friends myth is the idea some people have that girls are looking for a long-term relationship while boys are just interested in sex. This isn't necessarily how it really is. Sure, sometimes boys or girls are attracted to people strictly because of physical chemistry. But wanting to form a meaningful connection isn't exclusively a girl thing. Teens who've connected in this way will tell you that having a girlfriend or boyfriend who you care about, respect, and have fun being around can be one of the best relationships you'll ever have.

For a lot of people, being a part of a couple may be the first time they really become close friends with someone of the other sex. It gives them a chance to understand each other more. Being in a healthy boyfriend-girlfriend relationship can help get rid of some of those limiting gender roles. If the two people really like each other for who they are, it gives them the freedom to express both their feminine and masculine traits—traits they may feel they have to hold back when they're with other people.

Myth #2: If you are not dating yet, something must be wrong with you.

Reality check: Nothing is wrong with you. Some teens just aren't interested in dating yet. Because of family or religious values, they may see dating as an adult activity, one that only complicates a young person's life. Other teens may opt to concentrate on school, extracurricular activities, and community service projects—whatever it takes to get into the college or career training they want. And some teens just don't feel the need to rush. They're having plenty of fun hanging out and aren't ready for the commitment or responsibility of a relationship. They like having girls who are friends and boys who are friends. For these people, there'll be plenty of time for dating after graduation.

Myth #3: When a boy hangs out with girls, he's cool. When a girl hangs out with boys, she's easy.

Reality check: Being a girl and having friends who are boys and being a boy with friends who are girls can be great. However, sometimes the talk around school rewards boys for forming these kinds of friendships but restricts or punishes girls who form them. This idea came up often with teens who took our survey, particularly girls. One girl commented that if a girl spends time with lots of boys, "she's called a slut. But if a boy does it, everybody roots for him." Another girl wrote, "If guys talk to girls, they're just talking, but if girls talk to guys, they're flirting."

This is known as a double standard. Parents sometimes express it, too, but in a different way. They might be proud that their son has several "girl-friends" but worry their daughter will develop a "bad reputation." Is it fair? No. Don't buy into it. The number of boys or girls you hang out with or call, or who call you, doesn't make you cool, easy, or anything else. It's who you are, not who you're with, that counts.

Myth #4: Boys put out all the money. Girls have to pay them back somehow, right?

Reality check: Wrong. No one "owes" anyone sexual favors, and no one should be pressured or intimidated! That goes for boys who want to brag to their friends and for girls who want to brag to theirs. And guess what? Boys don't have to pay for everything. Girls have their own money, too. If you want to date someone but don't have the cash, find free or inexpensive things to do—like a walk in the park, a bike ride, a movie matinee, or a video. If you don't want to be seen as "owing" anyone, pay your way. And if you really like each other, share the expenses, or take turns paying.

A lot of times the things that complicate girlfriend-boyfriend relationships have to do with the way society thinks that teen boys and girls should act when they're a couple. Sometimes even people who are very confident about who they are will find themselves falling back on the old stereotypes when they start to date. Sometimes they may not even be aware of it.

Girl-boy relationships

What's different?

GIRLS	BOYS
• may feel they need to be sexy and beautiful to be interesting to a boy	• may feel they need to be strong and macho to be interesting to a girl
• may feel they should wait for the boy to call, that the boy should always pay, and that they shouldn't make the first physical move	• may feel they have to be the one to call, always offer to pay, and take the lead in a physical relationship

GIRLS

- may want lots of talking and regular attention
- may feel they need to go along with the boy and please him
- may feel they can't be assertive about what's okay and not okay

BOYS

- may want less talking and may not see the need to connect every day
- may feel pressure to have sex and therefore pressure the girl to do so
- may think a girl doesn't mean it when she says no

What's the same?

BOTH GIRLS AND BOYS

- may feel pressured into dating before they're ready or into dating someone they'd rather not
- may feel unsure of what's expected of them—not just by their boyfriend or girlfriend, but also by their friends or parents
- may feel they must choose or compromise their personal, family, or religious values about sex or risk losing their boyfriend's or girlfriend's continued affection or the respect of their friends
- want to know that the person they care about is loyal, honest, caring, understanding, supportive, and accepts them for who they are

Sex: Is everybody doing it?

Some teenagers have never been kissed or are taking it slow. Some have started experimenting sexually. A few are sexually active. Others are committed to abstinence and may have pledged not to have sex before marriage. Whatever you do or don't do, it's easy to feel that everyone is more experienced than you are or worry that you're the only person you know who's had a certain sexual experience.

Adding to this is the pressure that gets put on girls and boys by all those things we've talked about already: society, parents and other adults, songs, videos, TV, magazines, movies, friends, boyfriends, and girlfriends. Everybody is trying to tell you how boys and girls do, don't, should, or shouldn't behave when it comes to sex. And that doesn't even count the messages your own hormones are sending!

The boundaries society sets for boys and for girls surrounding sex are anything but clear. Take virginity, for example. A teen boy who is a virgin can be teased and harassed about it. Sometimes boys will even claim they've had sex when they really haven't, just to stop the teasing. On the other hand, a girl who's a virgin  might be called a "prude" or a "tease," while girls who have sex are often labeled "easy" or "sluts." In general, boys who have sex are respected while girls who have sex run the risk of being humiliated and ostracized. There's that double standard again.

You hear a lot about abstinence and safe sex—ways to prevent sexually transmitted diseases, infections, or pregnancy. (See pages 150–151 for resources that talk about sexual decision-making and safe sex.) But in terms of gender roles, there are issues of personal safety in romantic and/or sexual relationships. That myth that claims "when she says no, she really means yes" can be dangerous for both boys and girls. A boy may pressure a girl to go further sexually when she's not ready or doesn't want to. If he's older, bigger, stronger, more popular, or more powerful than she is, she may have trouble saying no. At the same time, a girl might believe that if she doesn't say no to *everything,* the boy will consider her a slut.

Why is this so confusing? One reason is those gender stereotypes people get in their heads—stereotypes that say (1) boys are supposed to have sex and have the right to be rough and tough and (2) girls really ask for sex when they wear a short skirt or halter top and really want sex even if they say no.

Of course, NOT all boys will pressure girls to have sex, and sometimes it's a girl putting pressure on the boy. Plenty of girls, too, are willing and able to be very clear about what they want. Many teenagers have caring relationships that are about a lot more than sex. And many couples enjoy holding hands and kissing without taking things any further.

As with friendships, respect is the key to a relationship with a girlfriend or boyfriend. If you are in a relationship where both people respect each other, where neither of you lets gender myths, stereotypes, and expectations get in the way, it will be easier to talk about these things and figure out what's right for you.

Keeping safe in relationships: 10 tips for girls and boys

Sexual pressures don't happen only in dating situations. Parties, concerts, post-game gatherings, and other social scenes can also turn risky. And girls aren't the only ones who are victims of unwanted sexual advances, sexual abuse, violence, and rape—boys can be, too. Here are some ways you can keep safe in your relationships.

1. Make sure you get together in a public place.

2. Don't go to parties alone. Always make sure you have people you trust along with you, especially if there'll be a clique present or a group of teens you hardly know, or if the ratio of boys to girls will be uneven, or if it turns out that there is alcohol or other drugs being used at the party.

3. Set personal boundaries before things get physical.

4. Remember that just because someone has paid for a movie or bought a gift doesn't mean he or she is entitled to sex. Just because someone acts or looks "sexy" doesn't mean she or he wants to have sex. Just because someone gets angry doesn't mean that you "made" the person act that way or that you deserve to be hurt or intimidated.

5. Drinking or using other drugs will get in the way of making good decisions . . . so don't use them and risk a poor decision.

6. Don't worry about hurting someone's feelings. If you're uncomfortable, clearly and firmly tell the person to stop. When someone says no to a sexual advance or tells you to stop, stop.

7. Just because someone doesn't want sex doesn't mean he or she is rejecting you as a person.

8. Be prepared in case something goes wrong. Have money or a cell phone so you can get another way home if necessary.

9. If the person you're with doesn't seem to respect you, respect yourself and look for a healthier relationship.

10. If something doesn't look, sound, or feel right, it probably isn't. Weigh the risks. Stay in control of your actions.

If someone is abusing you

If someone is physically or sexually abusing you, stop seeing the person and get help. Talk to your parents, a counselor, or another adult you trust. If you don't know who to talk to, call one of these 24-hour, toll-free numbers:

1-800-799-7233 (National Domestic Violence Hotline)

1-800-656-4673 (Rape, Abuse, and Incest National Network)

WHAT DO YOU THINK?

* What do you think makes a good boyfriend or girlfriend?

* What is a healthy dating relationship like? How can two people make this kind of relationship happen?

* When it comes to sex, what kinds of pressures do boys face? What kinds of pressures do girls face? How do you feel about these pressures?

Sexuality and gender

You may have heard the word *sexuality* and thought that it only applied to those people who have had sex. But you don't have to have had sex to be a sexual person. Everyone is sexual in one way or another.

Sexuality is about your senses, about the way you relate to the world as a teen girl or boy. It's about the way you see yourself and your body, and it's about the way you see and appreciate others. In a way, being sexy is about feeling good about yourself. Clothes can be sexy, a person's voice can be sexy, being smart can be sexy. Those things are all part of what draws you to others and what draws others to you.

It's hard to say exactly what you find attractive about another person. In Chapter 2 you looked at traits that are considered masculine or feminine. You may find both feminine and masculine qualities that are very attractive to you. Like gender, sexuality is on a continuum, with those so-called masculine and feminine traits at the far ends and a lot of room in the middle. All of the traits along the gender continuum can be sexy in people of either sex.

And sexuality isn't just physical—it's emotional, too. If you are really attracted to someone's sense of humor and great smile, you'll want to spend more time with that person. Yet that doesn't mean you necessarily want to be sexual with her or him.

WHAT DO YOU THINK?

* What are some traits that are considered feminine that you might find appealing in a boy?

* What are some traits that are considered masculine that you might find appealing in a girl?

Gay v. straight

We've talked about friendships, cliques, romance, and sex. But we haven't really gotten specific about one other important piece of the gender puzzle: straight, gay, and everything in between. You've probably seen the term "GLBT." What, exactly, does GLBT mean?

Let's back up and talk about "S" first. Women or men who are sexually attracted to people of the other sex are known as heterosexual or straight. If we gave these people a letter, it would be an "S," for straight. Men or women who are sexually attracted to people of the same sex are known as homosexual—gay or lesbian. Their letters are "G" or "L." Some people are sexually attracted to people of both sexes. These people are called bisexual or bi—"B." Some women feel more like men, even though they have a female body. And some men feel more like women, even though they have a male body. These people are known as transgender. That's what the "T" stands for.

It's not easy to be a teenager who is GLBT. These teens have a higher rate of depression and suicide than their heterosexual counterparts. This isn't because GLBT teens are inherently more depressed than their straight counterparts, but because they often endure a sense of isolation and feeling different, topped off by the way some people avoid, put down, or harass them day after day.

The term that refers to whether people are straight, gay, lesbian, bisexual, transgender, or a mixture of some of these is *sexual orientation*. Sexual orientation can get pretty confusing. Sometimes people who think they might be gay or bisexual really aren't. This is especially true for teens, who are in the process of discovering their sexuality. They might have a few experiences where they kiss or touch another person of the same sex in a sexual way, or have dreams or fantasies about people of the same sex. You might be surprised how many teens have confused feelings about whether they're straight or gay. Over time, people's sexual orientation becomes clear.

GENDER FACTS

* People do not choose to be gay or straight—they simply are.
* Experts believe that 10% of the U.S. population is gay or lesbian.

Sometimes when people are attracted to someone of the same sex, they may find that they begin to cut themselves off from the person they are drawn to, because they are afraid of their own feelings. They might worry that they are gay or that others will think they are gay. This can be especially troubling for boys because of the way society pressures them to be tough and macho. Many boys feel that nothing could be more feminine than being attracted to another male. Boys are sometimes so afraid that they might be gay, or that other people might think they're gay, that they avoid close relationships with other guys. Their friendships can't move beyond the surface because they are so afraid of what might happen if they let their guard down.

Often girls are more used to being close with their friends, to touching, hugging, and telling intimate secrets. But even girls have been known to call someone a "dyke" because the person doesn't dress like everybody else, or to feel threatened by the idea of being attracted to another girl.

These fears come from homophobia, which we talked about in Chapter 5 (pages 91–92). How many times have you heard a coach yell at his team for doing a poor job by calling them "ladies," "girls" or "sissies"? Or boys calling each other "fag" or "homo"? Or someone commenting on a particular hairstyle, action, answer, or look as "gay"? You might think homophobic comments like this are harmless, but they are actually hurtful. Imagine how it feels to hear these slurs when you are or think you might be gay or lesbian.

Putting stereotypes on people based on whether they're straight or gay is just as hurtful as stereotyping someone for being a girl or a boy. The more open you are to letting boys and girls be who they really are—rather than who gender stereotypes say they *should* be—the more accepting you will become toward all people of all sexual orientations.

GENDER FACT   Studies show that high school students hear anti-gay remarks as much as 25 times a day.

WHAT DO YOU THINK?

* Why do you think some people are afraid of those who are gay or lesbian?

* How do people in your school treat people who are GLBT?

* What are some things that you or your school could do to make it a place where GLBT students feel safe and respected?

Are you wondering if you're gay?

If you wonder whether you're gay, bi, or straight, it can be hard to figure this out. Just giving yourself time will probably show you the answer. But if you are struggling with the question and feel alone and confused, talk to an adult who can help, or call the National Youth Crisis Hotline's 24-hour, toll-free number: **1-800-448-4663.**

Every person of every sexual orientation has a particular, unique way of being a girl or a boy. Sexuality is part of gender, but it's only one part. Getting past those set roles, stereotypes, and expectations about gender really can make *all* your relationships stronger, more rewarding, and more fun.

"Boys and girls should be treated according to who they are, not what they are." Girl, 13

Find out more!

Cliques, Phonies, & Other Baloney by Trevor Romain (Minneapolis: Free Spirit Publishing, 1998). This is a humorous book that shows the ups and downs of popularity and cliques, and how to choose your own way to be part of a group.

The Guy Book: An Owner's Manual by Mavis Jukes (New York: Crown Publishers, 2002). Fun and information-packed, this book is billed as "Maintenance, Safety, and Operating Instructions for Teens." In chapters called "Under the Hood: Parts," "Sharing the Road: Girls," and "Road Hazards: Knowing Who and What to Avoid," you'll find lots of details and advice on topics from friendship to dating to sex.

It's a Girl Thing: How to Stay Healthy, Safe, and in Charge by Mavis Jukes (New York: Alfred A. Knopf, 1996). A reader-friendly book with lots of details about puberty, health issues, boy-girl relationships, sexuality, and safe sex.

The Teenage Guy's Survival Guide: The Real Deal on Girls, Growing Up, and Other Guy Stuff by Jeremy Daldry (Boston: Little, Brown and Company, 1999). This is a friendly, down-to-earth book that covers social life, love, and sex as well as body changes and the ups and downs of being a teenage boy.

Totally Me: The Teenage Girl's Survival Guide by Yvonne Collins and Sandy Rideout (Holbrook, MA: Adams Media Corporation, 2001). This book is full of information about friendships with girls, friendships with boys, and boyfriends. There's also a section on getting along with parents.

Boys and Girls Clubs of America
www.bgca.org
To get involved in peer mediation or other service-related activities, visit this site or check the White Pages for local Boys and Girls Clubs.

I Wanna Know
www.iwannaknow.org
This Web site of the American Social Health Association is easy to use and full of helpful information about all kinds of sex-related questions.

National Hotline for Gay, Lesbian, Bisexual and Transgender Youth
1-800-347-TEEN (1-800-347-8336)
This is a confidential hotline with youth counselors to answer questions and help teens find help. You can call from 7 to 10 P.M. CST Sunday–Thursday, and from 7 P.M. to 12 A.M. CST Friday and Saturday.

National Youth Crisis Hotline
1-800-448-4663
This 24-hour, toll-free hotline for youth in crisis situations is a program of Youth Development International. If you're under age 18, a runaway, struggling with drugs, physical abuse, rape, suicide, pregnancy, sexual pressure, or any other crisis, call this number for help and to be connected with options and referral services.

Parents, Families and Friends of Lesbians and Gays (PFLAG)
1726 M Street NW, Suite 400
Washington, DC 20036
(202) 467-8180
www.pflag.org
PFLAG is an organization for family members and friends of lesbian, gay, bisexual, and transgender individuals that offers support and education about gender identity and sexual orientation.

When Love Hurts
www.dvirc.org.au/whenlove
This Web site for teen girls is operated by the Domestic Violence and Incest Resource Center of Melbourne, Australia, and was the 2001 winner of the Australian Violence Prevention Award. Visit the site for information on relationship warning signs, sex and trust, healthy relationships, getting out of a relationship, helping a friend, and more.

YMCA
www.ymca.net
For more information about the YMCA nearest to you, use their national Web site to link to your local YMCA's site.

YWCA of the U.S.A.
www.ywca.org
(212) 273-7800
To find out more about the services and programs of the YWCA, or to find the YWCA closest to you, call or log onto their national Web site.

Chapter 8

BEYOND "BOY V. GIRL": FINDING THE REAL YOU

SURVEY COMMENTS:
How did students feel about being a boy or a girl?

 "I'm glad I'm a girl. The best thing is just making an impact by doing things people think you can't do, and you prove them wrong." —Girl, 14

"Being a boy? I enjoy it plenty—there's nothing I would change." —Boy, 15

"I like being a girl, but I would change things so we have more rights. I don't think we're equal enough." —Girl, 13

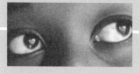 "I like being a boy. I think we have more freedom." —Boy, 15

"The worst thing is that I don't have much freedom like the boys do." —Girl, 15

"I don't like being a boy because there is too much responsibility." —Boy, 14

"Women have been through a lot to get where they are these days, and I'm proud of that and who I am." —Girl, 16

"I like being a guy. It's not necessarily fair, but I will make more money because of it." —Boy, 15

"I love being a girl. I can do anything." —Girl, 12

"I like being a boy because people respect you." —Boy, 13

"I like to be myself. If people like me, they do, and if they don't, they don't." —Girl, 13

"I am happy with who I am." —Boy, 14

Male? Female? What's really important?

Do you know yourself pretty well? Chances are you probably do. After all, you live with yourself 24/7. Knowing who you are can make you happier and more confident. It can help you figure out what's important to you about being a girl or a boy—the things you like and the things you'd like to be different. By moving beyond "boy v. girl" and discovering the real you underneath the layers of gender roles and expectations, you're taking a giant step toward getting past stereotypes to become the girl or boy you truly want to be.

Knowing yourself and liking yourself are closely connected. Most of the teens who took our survey—82 percent of both boys and girls—said they liked being the sex they were. What about you?

WHAT DO YOU THINK?

You considered these questions earlier in *Boy v. Girl?* Now see whether your answers have changed.

* Do you like being a girl or a boy? Why or why not?

* What do you think is the best part of being a boy or a girl? The worst part?

* If you could change anything about being a girl or a boy, what would it be?

People who took the survey wrote a lot about the things that are important to teenage boys and girls. Many of these teens thought some aspects of gender differences made sense, while others were wrong or silly. In reading nearly

2,000 surveys, we saw that society doesn't necessarily understand some of the things that are important to young people when it comes to gender.

What's important to teens?

- -

How society seems to see it

GIRLS CARE ABOUT

- clothes and makeup
- shopping
- relationships
- looks
- talking
- romance

BOYS CARE ABOUT

- cars
- sports and games
- competition
- strength
- being active
- sex

What society sometimes seems to forget

Not all girls or all boys think the same things are important. Boys and girls care deeply about a lot of the same things, including

- friends
- fairness
- the environment
- school
- creativity

- spirituality
- politics
- family
- self-confidence
- the future

- -

WHAT DO YOU THINK?

✴ What things under "How society seems to see it" are important to you? Why?

✴ If you could actually talk to "Society," what would you tell it you care about as a boy or a girl?

✴ What are some ways you can let people know what's important to you?

The things you do and care about will often be held up against the things society *thinks* you should do and care about. In other words, it might be easier to be (1) a girl who loves to shop rather than a girl who wants to take shop or (2) a boy who talks about sex and sports rather than a boy who talks about relationships and feelings.

It's true that society's assumptions about you, based on your sex, can be limiting. But we hope *Boy v. Girl?* has helped you become more aware that recognizing both the masculine and the feminine sides of yourself—and seeing the range of choices that are available to you—can increase your opportunities in life. Consider these ideas:

 A boy who believes (or who accepts society's belief) that boys always need to be tough may have difficulty asking for help or being sensitive to someone who needs his help. A girl who believes these things about boys may miss getting to know a lot of boys better. But if you're a boy *or* a girl who thinks it's great when boys can be tough, sensitive, or both, you'll have a better chance of getting along with more people and enjoying your relationships more.

A girl who believes (or accepts society's belief) that girls should always be quiet and agreeable might find it hard to stand up for herself when she really needs to. A boy who believes girls are weak or don't mean it when they say no may not figure out what's really going on with some of the girls he knows. But as a girl or boy who sees  that girls can be gentle, firm, or both, you'll go beyond gender stereotypes to get to know girls, and yourself, a whole lot better.

Being able to move between more "feminine" and "masculine" approaches to situations expands people's capabilities. Everybody needs to be strong sometimes. Everybody needs to be sympathetic and helpful at times, too. Why shouldn't all of these possibilities be open to all of us? Girl or boy, what's most important is respecting the different way each individual person can be. The ability to do this comes from respecting, knowing, and liking yourself.

Who are you?

What traits and feelings are basic to you? What makes you unique? Look again at the "Gender traits?" form on page 32:

1. If you have the copy you made and filled out when you read Chapter 2, look at it now. Would you still mark the same traits for girls and for boys? For you?

2. Choose three traits from the list that you think best describe you. (If you don't find the right traits on the list, use your own words.) How do you show the traits? You might write or talk about the traits by saying, "I would describe myself as _____ because _____."

3. Ask your friends to tell you which traits they think describe you, and why.

4. Talk about whether you think each trait is masculine, feminine, both, or neither. Would you or your friends use different words to describe you if you were the other sex?

Part of knowing yourself is knowing what's important to you. Think for a moment about your happiest memories. Those are probably moments when you were being most yourself. What can those memories tell you that's important now? Maybe you love soccer, and recall how excited you felt the first time you kicked a soccer ball down the field. Maybe another memory comes to mind, of having fun doing skits or plays. Could that still give you pleasure today? Do memories of chess games, building forts, working on a butterfly collection, or reading mysteries have to stay just memories? Are there things you once enjoyed that could lead you to new experiences now?

Be open to *all* of the real you. Explore it—let it shine through in as many ways as you can. It's harder for people to make assumptions about you when you're confident about who you are and what's important to you. Knowing these things can help you stand your ground when parents, teachers, friends, TV, and magazines try to tell you who you should be and what should be important to you. Plus, when you can begin to see yourself as a unique person—not the person other people say you are or who you think you ought to be because you're either a boy or a girl—you can also begin to see other people for who *they* really are.

As you get to know yourself better, you'll probably find things you want to change. Maybe you're very shy, and you'd like to be more outgoing. Maybe you have a tendency to speak before you think, and hurt people's feelings without meaning to. Maybe you avoid taking risks, and you'd like to be a little more adventurous.

Go back (yep, one more time!) to that "Gender traits?" list on page 32. This time, choose three things that *don't* describe who you are now but do describe ways you'd like to be sometime in the future. (If you don't find what you're looking for on the list, make up your own traits.) How can you work toward developing those qualities?

Here's a simple and effective way to get started. There used to be a TV commercial that showed crowds of people in a variety of places around the world. As you watched, one person on the screen held up a sign with two words on it: "I am." Soon other "I am" signs began to pop up, and you found yourself noticing particular people in the crowd because they were holding these signs. Behind the people, different words came across the screen, like *intelligent, creative,* and *capable.* And the people holding the signs suddenly did appear to be intelligent, creative, and capable. They seemed to have confidence. They looked like they knew what they were doing.

"I am." Those two little words have a lot of power. They can change the way you see yourself. What are the qualities that you'd like to develop? Imagine that you already have them. Now say each one aloud to yourself.

* "I am independent."

* "I am a good listener."

* "I am a leader."

Psychologists call these statements self-affirmations, or positive self-talk. To *affirm* means to declare something positively and firmly. So talk to yourself! Say these things several times a day. If you're having trouble starting with the words on your list, begin with something simpler, like "I am a unique individual." It may feel a little silly at first, because you're probably not used to saying good things about yourself, especially out loud.

It's so easy to believe messages that tell you you're not good enough, feminine enough, or masculine enough. Using affirmations is a way to quiet those negative voices, so that you can hear the positive things you have to say about yourself. Words alone may not make these things true, but they can help you see yourself in a new way, and help you find confidence to change and grow.

Another way to feel positive about yourself is to write a creed. A creed is a statement of what you believe. Sometimes people think creeds are religious. They can be, but anybody can write a creed about anything. The word creed comes from the Latin word *credere,* meaning "to believe." Stating your beliefs lets you formally say that you are a one-of-a-kind person who won't be held back by gender expectations and stereotypes.

To write your own creed, start with statements like these:

* As a girl, I believe I am . . . and that I can . . .

* As a boy, I believe I am . . . and that I can . . .

* As a human, I believe I am . . . and that I can . . .

Who do you want to become?

You can turn your affirmations and beliefs about who and how you want to be into goals. Some of your goals might be traits you want to develop and things you want to accomplish now or in the next few months or years. Others will be for later in your life. Have you thought about who you want to be and what you want to be doing when you're an adult? Imagining the future is often the first step toward making it a reality. It was one of the things we asked about in our survey.

THE SURVEY ASKED:

What do you imagine your life will be like when you're a man or a woman?

BOYS SAID:

"I will be a STAR, I hope."

"As I grow I will learn more and become more responsible for myself."

"I'll have a wife, a kid, and a good job."

"I have no clue."

"I imagine that I will be rich, and either be a basketball star, rapper, doctor, or record label owner."

"I will be a successful movie producer with a wife and kids."

"I'm scared. I want to stay in school forever."

"Things will be more complicated."

"The labels I have now will be gone."

"I imagine I'll be married to a smart woman and be an Egyptologist."

"I'm gonna make myself a good life."

GIRLS SAID:

"I will be successful and happy."

"I think I'll be a businesswoman and be very sophisticated."

"I'll be a good person and respect myself."

"I really can't imagine my future yet."

"I want to be a lawyer and have one child and a husband, and live in California or New York."

"What you look like won't matter as much as your personality."

"I will be totally self-reliant and owning my own things without any man's help."

"I think it will be rewarding and great."

"The guys will be more respectful."

"I'll be independent. I'll have my own house and I'll own my own company."

"Life will be very fun—a long adventure."

WHAT DO YOU THINK?

* What goals do you have for now? For as you get older?

* What are some ways you can start working to reach your goals?

This book has talked a lot about what society expects of boys and girls. But gender expectations apply to adults, too, and many people have ideas about what it means to be a man or a woman. These ideas can be very limiting. One place you can expect to encounter gender myths, stereotypes, and expectations is in the world of work. As one of the girls who took our survey wrote, "People don't like the idea of a female president or football player. They feel the same way about male ballerinas or nurses."

You know that gender roles have changed over the years, but how much? Here are some FAQs (frequently asked questions) from the teens we know.

Q: Isn't the idea of "men's work" and "women's work" a thing of the past?

A: While women and men have both moved into careers that were once considered inappropriate for their sex, things haven't changed as much as you might imagine. Eighty percent of women in the workforce are employed as administrative assistants (secretaries), salesclerks, nurses, and teachers. Women doing "men's work" (like construction) often have to work harder to prove that they're good enough to be doing the job. Plus, they typically get paid less than men doing the same job, and often have to deal with sexual harassment from coworkers. Men doing "women's work" (like nursing) also get harassed, and sometimes feel like they have to apologize for not having a more powerful job or one that makes more money.

Who works in which jobs?

These are U.S. government statistics on full-time workers for the year 2000.

JOB CATEGORY	WOMEN	MEN
secretaries	98.9%	1.1%
registered nurses	97.8%	2.2%

JOB CATEGORY	WOMEN	MEN
general office clerks	83.6%	16.4%
elementary school teachers	83.3%	16.7%
cashiers	77.5%	22.5%
retail and personal sales	63.5%	36.5%
secondary school teachers	57.9%	42.1%
cooks	43.3%	56.7%
architects	23.7%	76.3%
athletes	20.0%	80.0%
law enforcement officers	19.2%	80.8%
dentists	18.7%	81.3%
clergy	13.8%	86.2%
engineers	9.9%	90.1%
machinists	6.3%	92.7%
airplane pilots	3.9%	96.1%
construction workers	3.7%	96.3%

Q: Aren't there laws that say women have to be paid the same as men for the same work?

A: Yes, there are equal-pay laws, but they aren't always very well enforced. In 1998 the average male salary was $35,345, while the average female salary was $25,862. That's a difference of $9,438. It means that the average woman earns 73 percent of what the average male earns. Each year in the United States, a day is noted as Equal Pay Day. This is the day in that year when women have finally made as much money as men made by the end of the previous year. In the year 2000, that day fell on May 14—Mother's Day. On that day, women had worked sixteen and a half months to earn what men had earned in twelve months.

Pay differences

Here are more statistics for full-time workers for the year 2000.

JOB	WHEN MEN EARNED . . .	WOMEN EARNED . . .
retail and personal sales	$100.00	$55.80
sales supervisors	$100.00	$69.80
accountants and auditors	$100.00	$72.40
elementary school teachers	$100.00	$81.50
registered nurses	$100.00	$87.90
cashiers	$100.00	$88.20
secondary school teachers	$100.00	$88.60
cooks	$100.00	$89.50

In January 2000, President Clinton announced a plan to help close the wage gap between men and women and enforce equal-pay laws. Why does it take a special plan to enforce those laws? For one thing, people who do the hiring often have the legal right to decide what employees will be paid. They may make decisions based on circumstances such as a person's age, experience, and interview performance. A company can say that a wage is based on experience when really it's based on the employee's sex. This is just one example of what can happen even though there are laws in place to make things fair. To make equality a reality, everyone has to believe in it.

WHAT DO YOU THINK?

* Why do you think more women or more men hold some jobs?

* How do you think men's and women's jobs will change?

* Do you think it's fair for women and men to earn different pay for the same job? Why or why not?

* What kinds of gender barriers do you think you'll need to overcome to achieve your dreams?

Q: Don't men and women share housework and childcare more equally now than before?

A: The details about this aren't yet clear. Some studies seem to show that women still work harder at home, while others show men and women sharing work more evenly.

Two studies, two findings

- In one study, researchers at the University of Michigan found that women's household workloads increased by an average of four hours per week when they married or lived with men. The opposite was true for men, whose weekly household workloads were reduced by about three hours after they got married or moved in with a female partner. When a couple added children to the picture, women's workloads increased three more hours a week per child, while men's barely changed.

- In a different study, researchers at Radcliffe College found men in two-career families becoming more involved with raising children and dealing with household responsibilities. In this study, fathers with school-age children spent as many hours in childcare as mothers, and took on 45% of the household duties.

How do you think society expects women and men to act? What jobs does society say they should do? What *aren't* they "supposed" to do? Try this activity on your own or with a friend: Take a piece of paper and fold it in half vertically. At the top of one folded side write, "Where I live, women are 'supposed' to . . ." On the other side write, "Where I live, men are 'supposed' to . . ." Make two lists of the gender "rules" you think society sets for men and women. When you're done, unfold the paper and look at the lists side by side. What are the similarities and differences? Then write or think about how you want to be as an adult. How will you be like what society expects? How will you be different?

Where I live, men are "supposed" to:

Of course, adult roles have to do with more than jobs and household duties, even though people often focus on these kinds of activities when they talk about the future. How many times have you heard this question?

> **What do you want to be when you grow up?**

Probably more than you care to think about! But has anybody ever asked you this?

> **Who do you want to be now and in the future?**

That's a bigger—and in many ways more important—question. What do you think your life will be like when you're an adult? What do you want it to be like? What work will you do? Where will you live? Who will live with you? How will you spend a typical day? What do you think will be your most important accomplishment? As you think about these ideas, you might want to talk them over with a friend or someone in your family, too. You might even want to write a letter to yourself. Talk about who you are now and who you want to be in the months and years ahead. Tell yourself the dreams you have for your future. Share your hopes and fears for the kind of person you will become.

Finding role models

It's true that there are many inequalities. One hopeful sign we saw in the surveys, though, was in the number of teens who think boys and girls are equal—80 percent of the girls and 74 percent of the boys believe they are. It's also encouraging that there are many positive things happening in the world. There are people who live their lives with real respect for people of both sexes. There are also people who work actively to make the world a better place, by being courageous enough to step outside the stereotypical gender roles. Sometimes these people are working to help others be aware of the inequality that's out there. These people can be role models for you. They offer examples of how you can live a life that you are proud of.

Role models can come from all walks of life. They can be male or female, any age or any race. A role model can be someone you know, such as a person in your family, a teacher, a friend, or somebody from your neighborhood or place of worship. Role models can also be people you don't know personally, like an actor who refuses to play roles that glorify sex or violence, or an athlete who is both competitive and compassionate. You may find a role model who is successful in a career you're interested in pursuing. You may know of people from history who you consider role models as well.

Roles models aren't perfect. Like yourself, they learn from their mistakes and try not to repeat them. A positive role model is someone to look up to, someone to learn from, and someone to help you believe in yourself. Even if your role model is someone you can't talk to personally, having this person's example in your life is a constant reminder of what is possible.

WHAT DO YOU THINK?

* Who are some of your role models? Why do you admire each person?

* What do your role models show or teach you about your role as a boy or girl and as a human being?

* What do they show or teach you about your own role in the future?

Watching your words

One step you can take right now to show respect for yourself and others is to start being aware of the words you use. Language is a powerful part of gender stereotyping. *Gender-biased* language (words and phrases that use gender stereotypes or assumptions about gender roles) has been around for so long that you may not even be aware of the kinds of things you and other people are saying.

Rosalie Maggio has written several books about gender and language, including *Talking About People: A Guide to Fair and Accurate Language* and *The Nonsexist Word Finder*. Here are a few of the easy ways she suggests you can think about what you're saying.

Try not to use the word *he* to mean both he and she. This may seem pretty obvious, but it happens all the time. For example, imagine if we said, "We hope that by reading this book, a teenager will realize that he can be whatever he wants to be." That would make it sound like the book was written with mainly boys in mind, and not girls. One researcher estimated that the average person will hear the word *he* used this way over a million times in a lifetime. To include both boys and girls, we could instead say, "We hope that by reading this book, teenagers will realize that they can be whatever they want to be." Or, "We hope that by reading this book, you realize that you can be whatever you want to be."

Try not to use the words *man, men,* or *mankind* when you're referring to both women and men. Some people argue that when they use these words, everyone knows they're talking about both men and women. But the subtle message, the picture people form in their minds when they hear these terms, is male. Using the words *human beings* or *people* is more likely to give a picture of both women and men.

Try not to use a word that clearly refers to a male or a female in describing a job that both women and men can do. Would it make much sense to call the woman who delivers your mail a mailman? Or the man on the airplane who brings you a soda and helps you to your seat a stewardess? Here's a short list of gender-neutral words—words that apply to people of either sex without promoting gender stereotypes:

INSTEAD OF:	YOU CAN SAY:
jock	athlete
pom-pom girl	pom-pom twirler
cafeteria lady	cafeteria server, lunchroom worker
chairman/chairwoman	chair
waitress/waiter	server
actress	actor
ballerina	ballet dancer
policeman	police officer
fireman	fire fighter
mailman	mail carrier
stewardess	flight attendant
spokesman	representative
statesman	politician
congresswoman/congressman	legislator
businessman/businesswoman	executive, business person

Be polite. When it comes to language and gender, manners always count. Here are a few simple courtesies of language:

* Take turns. If you say "girls and boys" one time, say "boys and girls" the next time.

* Call people what they like to be called. This is especially true when it comes to titles like Mr., Ms., Miss, or Mrs.

* Put yourself in the place of the person you're speaking to. Whoever said "Sticks and stones may break my bones, but names will never hurt me" was probably never labeled a "sissy," "geek," "ditz," or "slut." Words *can* hurt. They can make you think less of yourself and others. But words can also be empowering and affirming. Just think how you feel when someone calls you cool, smart, attractive, talented, or totally amazing.

WHAT DO YOU THINK?

* Do you think the words you use have an effect on people's ideas about gender roles? Why or why not?

* What are some gender-biased words you or others use to describe people? What gender-neutral words could you use instead?

Working to change gender stereotypes

With this book, you've explored different ways gender affects your life, but how you use what you've learned is up to you. There are plenty of large and small ways you can work to change gender expectations and stereotypes. You can take action in your own life by paying attention to what you say and do and by focusing on who you want to be instead of who all those out-side influences seem to say you should be. You can talk to others about the inequalities in the ways boys and girls are treated and about how limiting gender stereotypes can be. You can even become socially active and organize with other people who want to make the world more gender-friendly for everyone. No matter where you start or how far you decide to go, the main thing is to do *something.* Here are some ways to begin:

* Recognize that the strongest relationships don't come from trying to be in control of someone, or feeling more or less smart or important than someone, or expecting someone to think and act "like a girl" or "like a boy." Healthy relationships start with respect. They develop when you work together and try to understand where the other person is coming from and what he or she is feeling.

* Make an effort not to think of violence as an option in the world or in your personal relationships. Violence can destroy a person's spirit and self-esteem. Violent teens can become violent adults. If anger is a problem for you, get help. (See pages 24–25 for more information on getting help for anger.)

* Learn to give to others. You can promote equality by learning to both take care of and rely on other people.

* Expect yourself to do things regardless of gender. Instead of thinking of something as a boy thing or a girl thing, ask yourself, "Is it a *me* thing? Is this something that works and feels right for *me?"*

WHAT DO YOU THINK?

Imagine a world without gender roles and stereotypes. It's twenty years from now, and you and all your friends have worked very hard to make the world a place where girls and boys are treated equally. In twenty years:

* What differences will there be in people's ideas about gender roles and stereotypes?

* How will your life be different?

* How will life be different for people of the other sex?

* What will be the best thing about the world?

One of the most effective things you can do to take action about what you've learned is to talk to others. If you're excited about making the world a better place for both boys and girls, you can get somebody else excited about it, too. Sometimes the easiest person to talk to is a close friend. You might ask your friend:

> Have you ever thought about what people think we should be like just because we're boys (or girls)?

> If there was one thing you could change about being a girl (or a boy) what would it be?

> Do you think boys and girls are equal at home and at school? Do they get treated the same? Do they treat each other the same?

> Have you ever thought about the way that teenage girls and boys are shown in magazines and on TV? Do you think people really think we're like that?

Maybe you've been taking action in what you see, what you say, and what you do, but you still want to do more. You don't have to wait until you're older to start making a difference in the world. You've probably had more than one teacher tell you that a verb is an "action" word. Here are some verbs for taking action at school and in your community.

Verbs for gender activists

* **Join** others who are working to stop labeling, excluding, and harassing and who want to start respecting, including, and appreciating other people who don't fit those male and female boxes people sometimes try to put them in.

* **Write** letters and send email to your school or town paper, the student council, the school board, and public officials letting them know when you feel your school or community is discriminating against some people based on gender stereotypes.

* **Speak up** about the positive and negative gender roles you see around you.

* **Circulate** petitions—to build a girls' football league, to start a coed dance group, to get more boys involved in the drama or poetry club.

* **Create** posters, flyers, and Web sites that celebrate what girls and boys have in common.

* **Walk, run, or bike** for a cause that you care about.

* **Volunteer** to help a candidate who cares about gender fairness get elected to student council or to a government office.

* **Believe** in yourself and the tremendous impact you and others like you can have in helping boys and girls, women and men live together safely and cooperatively in our world.

Finally, let yourself imagine. Imagine a world where people aren't judged based on whether they're male or female, where all possibilities are open to everyone. A world where people feel free to be themselves, accepted for who they are. Now imagine that you are in that world. If you can imagine it, you can make it happen.

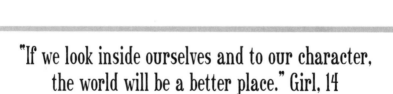

"If we look inside ourselves and to our character, the world will be a better place." Girl, 14

Find out more!

The Kid's Guide to Social Action: How to Solve the Social Problems You Choose—and Turn Creative Thinking into Positive Action by Barbara A. Lewis (Minneapolis: Free Spirit Publishing, 1998). Read this book to get inspired by stories of real kids who are making a difference all over the world. Then follow the book's step-by-step guides to taking social action in the ways you think are important.

What Do You Really Want? How to Set a Goal and Go for It! by Beverly K. Bachel (Minneapolis: Free Spirit Publishing, 2001). Whether you have short- or long-term goals, this book can help you set goals, work toward them, and get help in achieving them.

Do Something
423 West 55th Street, 8th Floor
New York, NY 10019
(212) 523-1175
www.dosomething.org
This Web site for teens offers all kinds of opportunities and ideas for how you can start taking action to change the world.

SHiNE (Seeking Harmony in Neighborhoods Everyday)
427 Broadway, Suite 41
New York, NY 10013
(646) 613-5100
www.shine.com
This is a national nonprofit organization that uses art, music, technology, and sports to engage and empower young people to take a stand, use their voice, and impact their world. SHiNE is the designated youth component of the White House's National Campaign Against Youth Violence. Its mission is to help young people develop the tools they need to build self-esteem, embrace diversity, promote social harmony, and practice nonviolence.

THE BOY SURVEY

Demographics

Your age:_____   Your race or ethnicity:_____

Where you live: (circle one)   URBAN AREA   SUBURB   SMALL TOWN   RURAL AREA   OTHER:_____

Gender Issues

1. What does the term gender mean to you? Please explain:

2. Do you think there are differences in how boys and girls think? Please explain:

3. Do you think girls and boys are equal? Why or why not?

4. Have you ever been stereotyped because of being a boy? Please explain:

continued

5. Do you ever stereotype others because they are boys or girls? Why or why not?

6. Do you think parents and teachers treat girls and boys equally? Why or why not?

7. Do most boys and girls have to follow the same rules at home or not? For example: Are their chores the same? Are their rules about clothes, curfews, or talking on the phone the same? Are they disciplined for the same things and in the same ways? Please explain your thoughts, using these or other examples:

8. Do authority figures at school expect the same behavior from both girls and boys? Please explain why you think they do or do not:

9. Think about your school's social scene: Are there any unwritten "rules" that seem to apply only to boys? If so, what are they?

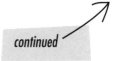

continued

10. Think about your school's social scene: Are there any unwritten "rules" that seem to apply only to girls? If so, what are they?

11. Think about a teen-related ad, magazine cover, music video, or movie you've seen. How did it portray boys or girls? Do you like this portrayal? Why or why not?

12. Do you feel that popular culture (things like TV, movies, magazines, music, and clothes advertising) affects people's ideas about what it means to be a boy? A girl? Does it affect your view? Please explain:

13. You know that girls and boys have different bodies—in what ways do these differences affect who they are? Please explain:

continued

More About You

14. Do you like being a boy? What are the best and worst things about it? What is the one thing you would change about being a boy? Please explain:

15. What do you imagine your life will be like when you're a man?

16. Have you ever been stereotyped because of your race or ethnic background? (circle one) YES / NO

17. If you have been stereotyped because of your race or ethnic background, were you stereotyped because of being a boy, too? Please explain:

18. If you have been stereotyped because of your race, ethnic background, and/or because you're a boy, please describe how you felt when this happened (or how you feel when this happens):

THE GIRL SURVEY

Demographics

Your age:_____ Your race or ethnicity:_____

Where you live: (circle one) URBAN AREA   SUBURB   SMALL TOWN   RURAL AREA   OTHER:_____

Gender Issues

1. What does the term gender mean to you? Please explain:

2. Do you think there are differences in how boys and girls think? Please explain:

3. Do you think girls and boys are equal? Why or why not?

4. Have you ever been stereotyped because of being a girl? Please explain:

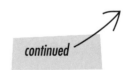

continued

5. Do you ever stereotype others because they are boys or girls? Why or why not?

6. Do you think parents and teachers treat girls and boys equally? Why or why not?

7. Do most boys and girls have to follow the same rules at home or not? For example: Are their chores the same? Are their rules about clothes, curfews, or talking on the phone the same? Are they disciplined for the same things and in the same ways? Please explain your thoughts, using these or other examples:

8. Do authority figures at school expect the same behavior from both girls and boys? Please explain why you think they do or do not:

9. Think about your school's social scene: Are there any unwritten "rules" that seem to apply only to girls? If so, what are they?

continued

10. Think about your school's social scene: Are there any unwritten "rules" that seem to apply only to boys? If so, what are they?

11. Think about a teen-related ad, magazine cover, music video, or movie you've seen. How did it portray boys or girls? Do you like this portrayal? Why or why not?

12. Do you feel that popular culture (things like TV, movies, magazines, music, and clothes advertising) affects people's ideas about what it means to be a girl? A boy? Does it affect your view? Please explain:

13. You know that girls and boys have different bodies—in what ways do these differences affect who they are? Please explain:

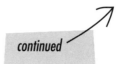

continued

More About You

14. Do you like being a girl? What are the best and worst things about it? What is the one thing you would change about being a girl? Please explain:

15. What do you imagine your life will be like when you're a woman?

16. Have you ever been stereotyped because of your race or ethnic background?
(circle one) YES / NO

17. If you have been stereotyped because of your race or ethnic background, were you stereotyped because of being a girl, too? Please explain:

18. If you have been stereotyped because of your race, ethnic background, and/or because you're a girl, please describe how you felt when this happened (or how you feel when this happens):

SOURCES FOR GENDER FACTS AND FIGURES

Page 11: The definition of stereotype is adapted from the American Heritage Dictionary, Second College Edition (Boston: Houghton Mifflin, 2000).

Pages 25–28: The information on the brain, thinking, and learning differences is adapted from several sources, including the work of Deborah Blum, Michael Gurian, and Susan Gilbert (see the bibliography for facts of publication), and Eric Chudler's Neuroscience for Kids Web site (see "Find Out More!" on page 31).

Page 35: The "Gender fact" is from "Home, School, and Playroom: Training Grounds for Adult Gender Roles" by Claire Etaugh and Marsha B. Liss, in *Sex Roles* 26, nos. 3/4 (1992), pages 129–144.

Page 62: Facts cited in "Before Title IX . . . and after" are from "Title IX: 25 Years of Progress" (U.S. Department of Education and the Office for Civil Rights, 1997).

Page 64: Facts cited in "At school" are from *Boys and Girls Learn Differently! A Guide for Teachers and Parents* by Michael Gurian and Patricia Henly, with Terry Trueman (San Francisco: Jossey-Bass, 2001); U.S. Department of Education, Office of Educational Research and Improvement, National Center for Education, *NAEP 1999 Trends in Academic Progress: Three Decades of Student Performance, NCES 2000-469,* by J.R. Campbell, C.M. Hombo, and J. Mazzeo (Washington, DC: U.S. Government Printing Office, 2000); U.S. Department of Education, National Center for Education Statistics, *Educational Equity for Girls and Women, NCES 2000-030,* by Yupin Bae, Susan Choy, Claire Geddes, Jennifer Sable, and Thomas Snyder (Washington, DC: U.S. Government Printing Office, 2000); U.S. Department of Education, National Center for Education Statistics, *Digest of Education Statistics 2000, Table 106* by Thomas Snyder (Baton Rouge, LA: Claitors Publishing Division, 2001); and "Student Subgroup Achievement on the NAEP 1997 Arts Assessment" by Sheida White and Alan Venneman, in *NAEP Facts,* vol. 4, no. 2, December, 1999.

Page 83: The "Gender fact" is from "Mythbusting: What Every Female Athlete Should Know" (Women's Sports Foundation, 2001).

Page 83: Statistic on cheerleading today in "A short history of boys, girls, and cheerleading" are from "NFHS Activities Participation Survey" (National Federation of State High School Associations, 1997).

Page 88: Facts in "Who participates?" are from "NFHS Activities Participation Survey" (National Federation of State High School Associations, 1997).

Page 92: The "Gender facts" are from *Hostile Hallways: Bullying, Teasing, and Sexual Harassment in School* (Washington, DC: American Association of University Women Educational Foundation, 2001) and *Making Schools Safe for Gay and Lesbian Youth* (Boston: Governor's Commission on Gay and Lesbian Youth, 1999).

Page 101: The statistics in "Media numbers" are from "Children and the Media: Reflections of Girls in the Media: A Two-Part Study on Gender and Media, Summary of Key Findings" (Children Now, 1997). This reports summarizes the results of two studies done by the Kaiser Family Foundation and Children Now and analyzed by Dr. Nancy Signorielli.

Page 128: The "Bully facts" are from *Youth Risk Behavior Surveillance System Summary* (Washington, DC: U.S. Department of Health and Human Services, 1999) and "Girls Just Want to Be Mean" by Margaret Talbot, in *The New York Times Magazine* (February 24, 2002), page 26.

Page 132: The "Clique facts" are from a poll conducted by Knowledge Networks for The Empower Program, sponsored by Liz Claiborne Inc. (February 2001).

Page 148: The "Gender facts" are from "Just the Facts About Sexual Orientation & Youth: A Primer for Principals, Educators & School Personnel" (1999), a publication endorsed by the American Academy of Pediatrics (AAP); and S. Brown, *Streetwise to Sex-Wise: Sexuality Education for High-Risk Youth* (Morristown, NJ: Planned Parenthood of Greater Northern New Jersey, 1993).

Page 149: The "Gender fact" is from K. Carter, "Gay Slurs Abound," in *The Des Moines Register* (March 7, 1997).

Pages 160–162: The information on jobs and pay rates for men and women, including the statistics in "Who works in which jobs?" and "Pay differences," comes from the U.S. Department of Labor, Bureau of Labor Statistics, cited in "20 Leading Occupations of Employed Women in 2000" and "Nontraditional Occupations for Women in 2000."

Page 163: The information in "Two studies, two findings" is from a study by Sanjib Gupta with the University of Michigan's Population Studies Center, presented at the American Sociological Association's annual meeting in 1998, and "Radcliffe Study Finds Decline of U.S. Family Exaggerated" in *The Harvard University Gazette* (June 13, 1996).

BIBLIOGRAPHY

The American Association of University Women, *How Schools Shortchange Girls: The AAUW Report* (New York: Marlowe & Company, 1995).

"An Annotated Summary of the Regulations for Title IX, Education Amendments of 1972" (The NOW Legal Defense and Education Fund, The Mid-Atlantic Equity Center and The NETWORK, Inc. 1993).

"Beyond Title IX: Gender Equity Issues in Schools" (The Mid-Atlantic Equity Center and the NETWORK, Inc. 1993).

Bingham, Mindy, Sandy Stryker, with Susan Allstetter Neufeldt. *Things Will Be Different for My Daughter: A Practical Guide to Building Her Self-Esteem and Self-Reliance* (New York: Penguin Books, 1995).

Blum, Deborah. *Sex on the Brain: The Biological Differences Between Men and Women* (New York: Viking Penguin, 1997).

Bornstein, Kate. *My Gender Workbook: How to Become a Real Man, a Real Woman, the Real You, or Something Else Entirely* (New York: Routledge, 1998).

"Boys to Men: Media Messages About Masculinity—Sixth Annual Children & the Media Conference Report " (Children Now, 1999).

"Boys to Men, Entertainment Media: Messages About Masculinity—A National Poll of Children, Focus groups, and Content Analysis of Entertainment Media" (Children Now, 1999).

Burke, Phyllis. *Gender Shock: Exploding the Myths of Male and Female* (New York: Anchor Books, 1996).

Caseau, David L., Ruth Luckasson, and Roger L. Koth, "Special Education Services for Girls with Serious Emotional Disturbance: A Case of Gender Bias?" *Behavioral Disorders,* 20: 1 (1994), pages 51–60.

Gardner, Howard. *Intelligence Reframed: Multiple Intelligences for the 21st Century* (New York: Basic Books, 1999).

Gilbert, Susan. *A Field Guide to Boys and Girls: Differences, Similarities: Cutting Edge Information Every Parent Needs to Know* (New York: HarperCollins, 2000).

Gurian, Michael. *A Fine Young Man: What Parents, Mentors and Educators Can Do to Shape Adolescent Boys into Exceptional Men* (New York: Jeremy P. Tarcher/Putnam, 1998).

Gurian, Michael, Patricia Henley, with Terry Trueman. *Boys and Girls Learn Differently! A Guide for Teachers and Parents* (San Francisco: Jossey-Bass, 2001).

"Hostile Hallways: Bullying, Teasing, and Sexual Harassment in School" (Washington, DC: American Association of University Women Educational Foundation, 2001).

Hughes, Jean O'Gorman and Bernice R. Sandler. "'Friends' Raping Friends—Could It Happen to You?" (Washington, DC: Project on the Status and Education of Women, Association of American Colleges, 1987).

Kaser, Joyce and Susan Shaffer, "It's Your Right!" (The NETWORK, Inc., 1995).

Kindlon, Dan, Michael Thompson, with Teresa Barker. *Raising Cain: Protecting the Emotional Life of Boys* (New York: Ballantine Books, 1999).

Koss, Mary P., Lisa A. Goodman, Angela Browne, Louise F. Fitzgerald, Gwendolyn Puryear Keita, Nancy Felipe Russo. *No Safe Haven: Male Violence Against Women at Home, at Work and in the Community* (Washington, DC: American Psychological Association, 1994).

Maggio, Rosalie. *Talking About People: A Guide to Fair and Accurate Language,* 3rd Edition (Phoenix, AZ: Oryx Press, 1997).

Miedzian, Myriam. *Boys Will Be Boys: Breaking the Link Between Masculinity and Violence* (New York: Anchor Books, 1991).

"Myth Busting: What Every Female Athlete Should Know!" (East Meadow, NY: Women's Sports Foundation, 2001).

Nelson, Mariah Burton. *Are We Winning Yet? How Women Are Changing Sports and Sports Are Changing Women* (New York: Random House, 1991).

NiCarthy, Ginny. *Getting Free: You Can End Abuse and Take Back Your Life,* 15th Anniversary Edition (Seattle, WA: Seal Press, 1997).

Orr, Donald P., and Gary M. Ingersoll. "The Contribution Level of Cognitive and Pubertal Timing to Behavioral Risk in Young Adolescents," *Pediatrics*, 95: 4 (April 1995), pages 528–533.

Pipher, Mary. *Reviving Ophelia: Saving the Selves of Adolescent Girls* (New York: Ballantine Books, 1995).

Pollack, William S., with Todd Shuster. *Real Boys' Voices* (New York: Random House, 2000).

"Reflections of Girls in the Media: A Two-Part Study on Gender and Media, Summary Key Findings" (Children Now, 1997).

"Reflections of Girls in the Media: Fourth Annual Children & the Media Conference Report" (Children Now, 1997).

Signorile, Michael Angelo. *Outing Yourself: How to Come Out as Lesbian or Gay to Your Family, Friends, and Coworkers* (New York: Random House, 1995).

Stepp, Laura Sessions. *Our Last Best Shot: Guiding Our Children Through Early Adolescence* (New York: Riverhead Books, 2001).

Strauss, Susan, with Pamela Espeland. *Sexual Harassment and Teens: A Program for Positive Change* (Minneapolis: Free Spirit Publishing, 1992).

Tannen, Deborah. *You Just Don't Understand: Women and Men in Conversation* (New York: Quill, 2001).

Thompson, Michael, Catherine O'Neill Grace, with Lawrence J. Cohen. *Best Friends, Worst Enemies: Understanding the Social Lives of Children* (New York: Ballantine Books, 2001).

"Title IX: 25 Years of Progress" (U.S. Department of Education and the Office for Civil Rights, 1997).

INDEX

Reproducible pages are in **bold**.

Y

ABOUT THE AUTHORS

George Abrahams, Ph.D., is a psychologist who has specialized in working with children, adolescents, and families for over twenty years. He has worked and consulted with schools, hospitals, and other community-based programs in addition to maintaining a private practice. George has a longstanding interest in adolescence and gender-role issues and has received a number of grants to promote school-based programming for teenagers.

Sheila Ahlbrand is a freelance writer and the Director of Children, Youth, and Families at a church in downtown St. Paul, Minnesota. She is the former Associate Director of the Upper Midwest Women's History Center, where she wrote and developed curriculum, and a former teacher with the Head Start Program. As an actress, Sheila toured parts of the Midwest with the Bridgework Theatre Company, presenting programs on sexual-abuse prevention to elementary and junior high audiences.

Other Great Books from Free Spirit

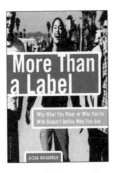

More Than a Label
Why What You Wear or Who You're With Doesn't Define Who You Are

by Aisha Muharrar

Preppy. Techie. Geek. Freak. Goth. Jock. These are just a few of the labels teens endure every day. Written by a teen, this book empowers students to stand up for themselves and understand others. Drawing from surveys from more than 1,000 teens ages 13–17, from small towns, suburbs, and rural areas across the U.S.A., this book reveals how labels define, limit, stereotype, and hurt. For ages 13 & up.

$13.95, softcover, illust., 152 pp., 6" x 9"

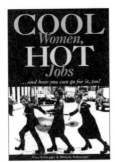

Cool Women, Hot Jobs
. . . and how you can go for it, too!

by Tina Schwager and Michele Schuerger

Women with great jobs tell their personal stories—and readers learn how to pursue their own "hot jobs." This book is filled with ideas, information, resources, activities, and journaling exercises readers can use to plan and pursue their own dreams. Upbeat, fact-filled, rich in personal experiences and sound advice for any girl or young woman who wants an exciting and meaningful future. For ages 11 & up.

$15.95, softcover, B&W photos, 288 pp., 6" x 9"

You're Smarter Than You Think
A Kid's Guide to Multiple Intelligences

by Thomas Armstrong, Ph.D.

Thomas Armstrong tells readers how to use all eight intelligences in school, build them at home, and draw on them to plan for the future. Resources describe related books, software, games, and organizations. As kids read the book, try the ideas, and check out the resources, they stop asking "How smart am I?" and start asking "How am I smart?" For ages 8–12.

$15.95, softcover, illust., 208 pp., 7" x 9"

Too Old for This, Too Young for That!
Your Survival Guide for the Middle-School Years

by Harriet S. Mosatche, Ph.D., and Karen Unger, M.A.

Finally there's a survival guide for the "tweens." Comprehensive, interactive, friendly, and fun, meticulously researched and developmentally appropriate, this book addresses issues that matter to young people this age. Packed with quizzes, anecdotes, stories, surveys, and more, this is just what boys and girls need to make the most of middle school—and beyond. For ages 10–14.

$14.95, softcover, illust., 200 pp., 7" x 9"

Bringing Up Parents

The Teenager's Handbook

by Alex J. Packer, Ph.D.

Straight talk and specific suggestions on how teens can take the initiative to resolve conflicts with parents, improve family relationships, earn trust, accept responsibility, and help to create a happier, healthier home environment. For ages 13 & up.

$15.95, softcover, illust., 272 pp., 7¼" x 9¼"

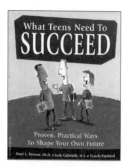

What Teens Need to Succeed

Proven, Practical Ways to Shape Your Own Future

by Peter L. Benson, Ph.D., Judy Galbraith, M.A., and Pamela Espeland

Based on a national survey, this book describes 40 developmental "assets" all teens need to succeed in life, then gives hundreds of suggestions teens can use to build assets at home, at school, in the community, in the congregation, with friends, and with youth organizations. For ages 11 & up.

$14.95, softcover, illust., 368 pp., 7¼" x 9¼"

Stick Up for Yourself!

Every Kid's Guide to Personal Power and Positive Self-Esteem

Revised and Updated

by Gershen Kaufman, Ph.D., Lev Raphael, Ph.D., and Pamela Espeland

Realistic, encouraging, how-to advice for kids on being assertive, building relationships, becoming responsible, growing a "feelings vocabulary," making good choices, solving problems, setting goals, and more. For ages 8–12.

$11.95, softcover, illust., 128 pp., 6" x 9"

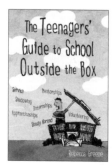

The Teenagers' Guide to School Outside the Box

by Rebecca Greene

This practical, inspiring book explores the world of alternative learning, giving teens the knowledge and tools they need to make good choices. Rebecca Greene introduces and describes a world of possibilities, from study abroad to internships, apprenticeships, networking, job shadowing, service learning, and many more. For ages 13 & up.

$15.95, softcover, illust., 272 pp., 6" x 9"

School Power
Study Skill Strategies for Succeeding in School
Revised and Updated Edition
by Jeanne Shay Schumm, Ph.D.
This popular study-skills handbook, newly revised and updated, covers everything students need to know, including how to get organized, take notes, do Internet research, write better, read faster, study smarter, follow directions, handle long-term assignments, and more. For ages 11 & up.
$16.95, softcover, B&W photos and illust., 144 pp., 8½" x 11"

What Do You Stand For?
A Kid's Guide to Building Character
by Barbara A. Lewis
Young people need guidance from caring adults to build strong, positive character traits—but they can also build their own. This inspiring book invites them to explore and practice honesty, kindness, empathy, integrity, tolerance, patience, respect, and more. For ages 11 & up.
$19.95, softcover, B&W photos and illust., 284 pp., 8½" x 11"

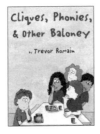

Cliques, Phonies, & Other Baloney
by Trevor Romain
Written for every kid who has ever felt excluded or trapped by a clique, this book blends humor with practical advice as it tackles a serious subject. For ages 8–13.
$9.95, softcover, illust., 136 pp., 5⅛" x 7"

To place an order or to request a free catalog of SELF–HELP FOR KIDS® and SELF–HELP FOR TEENS® materials, please write, call, email, or visit our Web site:

Free Spirit Publishing Inc.
217 Fifth Avenue North • Suite 200 • Minneapolis, MN 55401-1299
toll-free 800.735.7323 • local 612.338.2068 • fax 612.337.5050
help4kids@freespirit.com • www.freespirit.com

Visit us on the Web!
www.freespirit.com

Stop by anytime to find our Parents' Choice Approved catalog with fast, easy, secure 24-hour online ordering; "Ask Our Authors," where visitors ask questions—and authors give answers—on topics important to children, teens, parents, teachers, and others who care about kids; links to other Web sites we know and recommend; fun stuff for everyone, including quick tips and strategies from our books; and much more! Plus our site is completely searchable so you can find what you need in a hurry. Stop in and let us know what you think!

Just point and click!

new! Get the first look at our books, catch the latest news from Free Spirit, and check out our site's newest features.

contact Do you have a question for us or for one of our authors? Send us an email. Whenever possible, you'll receive a response within 48 hours.

order! Order in confidence! Our secure server uses the most sophisticated online ordering technology available. And ordering online is just one of the ways to purchase our books: you can also order by phone, fax, or regular mail. No matter which method you choose, excellent service is our ultimate goal.

1.800.735.7323 • fax 612.337.5050 • help4kids@freespirit.com